Praise for New Direction
Relational Ground, Authe

MW01153446

"With *New Directions in Gestalt Group Therapy*, Peter Cole and Daisy Reese have made an important contribution to gestalt therapy's growing library of clinical and theoretical literature. Cole and Reese's integration of gestalt and group therapy principles opens up new avenues of thinking and introduces methodological advances that will be highly relevant to all gestalt therapists who work with groups—whether they work as practitioners, trainers, or organizational consultants. Deeply personal in parts, and interlaced throughout with rich clinical material, this book is the product of mature clinicians who approach theory with sophistication and creativity. I recommend it to all gestalt therapists who work with groups."

Gary Yontef, PhD, author of *Awareness, Dialogue and Process: Essays on Gestalt Therapy* (Gestalt Journal Press, 1988) and co-founder and senior faculty member of the Pacific Gestalt Institute

"This is a well-written, wonderful weaving together of solid gestalt therapy theory and modern group therapy principles, including the all-important systems theory. I thoroughly enjoyed reading it. The clinical material was interesting and helpful in elucidating the theory. After running groups and teaching group therapy for almost five decades, I found much to think about for my own practice and teaching. The authenticity, humanness, and mastery of Daisy and Peter shine throughout. I especially appreciated the various quotes—and the Afterword commenting on the election of Donald Trump. I feel strongly that those of us with an understanding of group dynamics have much to say to our fellow citizens at this time in our country's history."

Maryetta Andrews-Sachs, LICSW, CGP, FAGPA, faculty (former dean and chair), Washington (DC) School of Psychiatry National Group Psychotherapy Institute, and past president, Mid-Atlantic Group Psychotherapy Society

"I love this whole book! It will be so useful to the world of group facilitators and the world of gestalt practice. Peter and Daisy speak with a lovely balance between theory, pragmatics, and examples: breaking new ground, they elaborate the shadow side of group dynamics in a way that expands our maps and our capacities to meet each other more fully and humanly while also calling our attention to the importance of the "experienced cultural influences" and capacities for gestalt group therapy to impact social change. A great new contribution."

Mary Ann Kraus, PsyD, co-chair of the Groups Facilitation Training Program, Gestalt Institute of Cleveland

"This new book of Peter Cole and Daisy Reese is another step in moving beyond the hot seat to group processes, integrating gestalt ideas of awareness, contact, and presence that focus on the individual with field theory forces that relate to the group-as-a-whole. In today's digital world with its virtual connections, the idea of contact and the importance of embodiment, so central in gestalt theories and gestalt group therapy, seem obsolete. Peter and Daisy remind us that without contact we lose our meaningful attachment to one another. The relational emphasis of the writers puts this book at the cutting edge in the field of psychotherapy. I recommend this book both to therapists who do not know enough about gestalt group therapy and to gestalt colleagues who want to deepen their understanding in this field."

Haim Weinberg, PhD, co-author of *The Social Unconscious in Persons, Groups, and Societies* (Karnac Books, 2010), and past president of the Israeli Association of Group Psychotherapy and the Northern California Group Psychotherapy Society

"*New Directions in Gestalt Group Therapy* does a fine job both of elaborating the theory of gestalt group therapy and of inviting the reader to the experience of *what it is* to participate in such groups. At the same time, this book goes beyond the sometimes-limiting boundaries of gestalt therapy, introducing the reader to the wider view and values that the gestalt philosophy of being entails. The authors remind us that there is a part of each person that sometimes is in need of help. They invite the reader to find hope both personally and collectively through connectedness and relationship. This book reminds us that all humans survive and thrive in groups, and the quality of our lives depends on our ability to co-exist as peacefully and respectfully as possible."

Dr Talia Bar-Yoseph Levine, president elect of the Association for the Advancement of Gestalt Therapy and editor of *The Bridge: Dialogues across Cultures* (Gestalt Institute Press, 2005) and *Gestalt Therapy: Advances in Theory and Practice* (Routledge, 2011)

"This clearly written book is an invaluable resource for clinicians of any theoretical orientation. It is packed with a wealth of essential information for beginning professionals as well as for seasoned therapists, and a must-read for students and those in training. I highly recommend it to anyone interested in deepening their knowledge and understanding of group work, and how groups work!"

Eva Gold, PsyD, co-director of the Gestalt Therapy Training Center-Northwest and author of *Buddhist Psychology* and *Gestalt Therapy Integrated: Psychotherapy for the 21st Century* (in press)

New Directions in Gestalt Group Therapy

Gestalt therapists often work with groups. Group therapists from a variety of theoretical orientations frequently incorporate insights and methodology from gestalt therapy. *New Directions in Gestalt Group Therapy: Relational Ground, Authentic Self* was written paying particular attention to both gestalt and group work specialists to provide a comprehensive reference for the practice of group therapy from a gestalt perspective. It includes an introduction to gestalt therapy terms and concepts written to make the gestalt approach understandable and accessible for mental health practitioners of all backgrounds. It is appropriate for students as well as seasoned psychotherapists.

Peter Cole and Daisy Reese are the co-directors of the Sierra Institute for Contemporary Gestalt Therapy located in Berkeley, California. They are the co-authors of *Mastering the Financial Dimension of Your Psychotherapy Practice* and *True Self, True Wealth: A Pathway to Prosperity*. They are a married couple, with five children and four grandchildren between them.

Peter H. Cole, LCSW, CGP, is in private practice in Berkeley and Sacramento, California. He is an assistant clinical professor of psychiatry with the Univeristy of California Davis School of Medicine, where he has taught gestalt therapy for over 25 years. He has taught group therapy at the Stanford University School of Medicine, the Wright Institute (Berkeley) and the Psychotherapy Institute (Berkeley). He is a graduate of the Washington School of Psychiatry's National Group Psychotherapy Institute. He is a certified group psychotherapist (American Group Psychotherapy Association) as well as a certified gestalt therapist (Pacific Gestalt Institute). Peter is also a Chartered Financial Consultant® who specializes in serving clients with social and environmental concerns.

Daisy Reese, LCSW, CGP, is in private practice in Berkeley and Sacramento, California. She has taught group therapy at the Wright Institute and the Psychotherapy Institute (both in Berkeley). She is a graduate of the Washington School of Psychiatry's National Group Psychotherapy Institute and is a certified group psychotherapist (American Group Psychotherapy Association). She is past president of the Northern California Group Psychotherapy Society.

New Directions in Gestalt Group Therapy

Relational Ground, Authentic Self

Peter H. Cole and Daisy Reese

Routledge
Taylor & Francis Group

NEW YORK AND LONDON

First published 2018
by Routledge
711 Third Avenue, New York, NY 10017

and by Routledge
2 Park Square, Milton Park, Abingdon, Oxon OX14 4RN

Routledge is an imprint of the Taylor & Francis Group, an informa business

Cover illustration by Eugenia Petrovskaya

Library of Congress Cataloging-in-Publication Data
A catalog record for this book has been requested.

ISBN: 978-1-138-94861-7 (hbk)
ISBN: 978-1-138-94862-4 (pbk)
ISBN: 978-1-315-66954-0 (ebk)

Typeset in Sabon
By Out of House Publishing

We dedicate this book to our family. Our children and their partners, Ananda and Joe, Reese and Faith, Alex and Katy, Elizabeth and Danny, and Hannah and James, are beautiful people with whom we love experiencing all of life's joys, challenges, and seasons. Our grandchildren, Sammy, Rowan-Hays, Eleanor, and Jack, light up our lives. Peter's mom, Joan Cole, at 87 years old, is passionate about her continuing work as a gestalt therapist, has provided insightful feedback on early drafts of this book, and has been a consistent source of emotional support. Thank you all for being the most loving family we could possibly ask for.

Contents

Foreword

This book is embedded in what Peter Cole and Daisy Reese have called the "grand journey in a caravan peopled with seekers of truth, authenticity, and connection." While carefully and extensively spelling out a range of the gestalt therapy principles, they humanize these principles by telling a story of the lives their therapy groups exemplify. Such attention given to ordinary human feelings and purposes takes the reader beyond the boundaries of psychopathology that often dominate the therapeutic literature. By vitalizing the breadth of personal existence, the authors create a fertile atmosphere of mutuality and discovery. They weave the life experiences of their group members in and out of theoretical guidelines. For the professional therapist, this lights up a recognizable pathway to help people recover displaced aspects of personal relationship. These principles provide a scaffold for reconstructing diminished personal effectiveness, stimulating people to revisit stories of miscast bargains they live with. The abundance of storyline gives immediacy to the struggle of people who have sacrificed vitality and relationship so as to soften the pain of contradiction and abandoned purpose.

In this journey, the authors guide the reader to many of those specifics of gestalt therapy that introduce group members to a life of possibility. In a group atmosphere of connectedness and belonging, they light up the lessons that reveal previously blurred beauty, hidden by a lifetime of habits and familiarity. Yes, connectedness and belonging are keys to the group arousal, enveloping them into a safe experiment with good living. The convergence of group members' attention creates a sense of enhanced personal identity and a commonly felt enchantment.

There are far-reaching implications of the authors' relational emphasis. The highlighting of connectedness and belonging, fundamental to living, honors the power of group members to provide a non-professional therapeutic effect. This communal contribution each person may offer the others is a serendipitous augmentation. It not only enlarges the work of therapeutic authority but also promises to widen the relevance of group therapy. In a society seeking maximal function of each person, the task of the therapist is a highly developed discipline multiplying a fundamental skill available to everyone. We are all on the edge of being experts in living. The increase in each person's search for a secure vitality is a step beyond the medical purpose of dissolving personal disturbance. That is, the conversations among group members and the insights they achieve are amply reported in this book and reveal the recovery of wisdom. These expansions of personal perspective join the original curative purposes. They offer a surprising relief of disturbance by inspiring people to look freshly at themselves and others. To live well is the ultimate wish that is always implicit in the role of group therapy, which seeks to expand anyone's life vista. By accepting the basics of personhood shared by everyone, the feeling that we are all in this together is not only comforting but also responsive to a basic human reflex. In gestalt therapy theory, the basic principle is that all experience is made up of figure and ground. Nothing is experienced all by itself. People experience nothing as an entity alone. Indeed, everything is inevitably embedded in an enveloping context. This principle, accordingly, points us to the fact that people innately wish to connect with each other and to identify with a group to which they belong.

Such a move—to honor both self and other—requires considerable savvy. The skill and opportunity required are all tapped in the therapy group environment. This transcendence beyond ordinary curative purpose into the more poetic, lyrical aspects of living is well reflected by Cole and Reese (p. 165):

> *The journey to aliveness, engagement in the world, risk-taking and connectedness is the grandest journey of all. And like all archetypal journeys, it can be terrifying at times. It involves contending with each other in group, grappling with our demons, being lost, getting found, experiencing rupture and repair. We need each other to do this work, which is hallowed by the group that confronts us, challenges us, cries with us, laughs with us, calls us to account, and most importantly, belongs to us: passionately counting us as one of its members, and refusing to give up on us, even when we have shown the parts of ourselves of which we are the most ashamed.*

Yes, indeed, this book takes its place in the expansion of cultural orientation and guidance, honoring the human spirit. This is represented in the ordinary concerns of everyday people. They are the people, amply illustrated in this book, honored by simple recognition of the inspirational qualities of people connecting with people. In the face of hidden dangers that linger everywhere, they help to navigate through this abundance of human experience. We see in this journey the beauty that is haunted by the indivisible dangers residing in the human vista. One is grateful for Cole and Reese, who serve as wise guides keeping a vigilant eye out for the intrusions that interfere with simple blessedness.

Erving Polster 2017

Acknowledgments

We would like to thank the wonderful people at Routledge. It is a blessing to have a long-standing relationship with a publisher for whom we have such deep respect. We thank our editor, Elizabeth Graber, with whom we worked on an earlier book, for her support, enthusiasm, and professionalism as we brought this book to fruition. We thank Nina Guttapalle for her editorial excellence. Also at Routledge, we would like to thank Dr. George Zimmar, who, 15 years ago, took a cold call from us—totally unknown, unpublished writers—as we pitched to him a book idea: *Mastering the Financial Dimension of Your Psychotherapy Practice*—upon which he ultimately took a chance. George, the opportunity you afforded us truly changed our lives!

We would like to thank our editorial assistant, Sarah Jenkins, for her help in getting the manuscript for this book in shape for submission to Routledge. From the moment we connected with you, Sarah, your dedication to this project has been total. Thank you!

Thanks to Peter deLeeuw for his generous, thoughtful, and insightful feedback on this manuscript. We've been friends since we were kids and you have always amazed me (Peter) with your kindness and brilliance.

Many thanks to Bud Feder for his close editing of Chapters 2 and 4. Being edited by you is a truly intimate and uplifting experience, Bud. You get it, you sharpen it, and you raise it to the next level. And many thanks to Jack Aylward for his outstanding editing of Chapter 4.

To our invaluable office manager, Shila Vardell, who consistently sounds a grounding and reassuring note of sanity in the midst of chaos—we don't really have the words to express the depth of our appreciation, so we will just say "Thank you, Shila, for all you do!"

Four Notes to Our Readers

On Gender and Pronoun Usage in this Book

In an effort to include people of all genders, we have adopted the occasional use of the singular "they" as a non-binary pronoun. While this wording might sound awkward at first to some readers, we feel that it is appropriate for a book on gestalt group therapy, a form of psychotherapy that deeply values diversity.

On Authorship

Peter Cole and Daisy Reese have co-written all the chapters of this book. However, some chapters were written in either Daisy or Peter's first-person voice. At the beginning of each chapter, we will make note of whether it is written in Daisy's voice, Peter's voice, or both.

On Clinical Vignettes and Client Anonymity

Throughout this book we present a variety of clinical vignettes. All clinical vignettes are thoroughly fictionalized, bringing forth clinical themes while protecting client confidentiality by creating purely fictional characters and situations.

On "Gestalt Group Therapy" and Its Acronym "GGT"

Throughout this book we will use the term "gestalt group therapy" and its acronym "GGT" interchangeably.

Introduction

Gestalt Group Therapy: A Robust Approach for the Challenges of 21st Century Psychotherapy

This introduction is written in the voices of both Peter and Daisy

Gestalt group therapy (GGT) provides a robust, theoretically rich, and methodologically sound framework for 21st century group therapy. As we will see in the ensuing chapters, GGT's holistic, field-centered approach allows the therapist to hold the therapy group with breadth and depth. GGT has the breadth to address social and political concerns that arise in the therapy group, along with the depth to support the emotional growth and development of group members while concurrently offering an experience of human connection and community.

Gestalt therapy is a humanistic system of psychology that grew historically out of the rich tapestry of European intellectual life in pre-World War II Germany, with its roots in progressive psychoanalysis, gestalt psychology,[1] field theory, phenomenology, and Martin Buber's ([1923] 1970, 1992) philosophy of dialogue (Bocian, 2010). The political and social devastation caused by fascism and the resulting diaspora of European intellectual life was the chaos from which gestalt therapy emerged in the early 1950s in New York City. GGT has the rich history, theory, and creative methodology that today's group therapists need to assist their clients with the many challenges they face.

Our intention with this book is twofold. First, we seek to describe, explain, and communicate the approach to gestalt group therapy that we have been practicing and honing for over 25 years. This involves the application of gestalt therapy theory and methodology to the interactive, process-oriented group situation. In so doing, we have developed some new ideas and ways of looking at both gestalt therapy and group therapy. Second, we seek to present the elegance of gestalt therapy theory to group therapists who may not be familiar with the gestalt approach. This task is an exciting and daunting one for us. We hope that gestalt therapists will gain a greater understanding of how to work with the group interactively, and that group therapists who practice from other theoretical orientations will be enriched by their exposure to gestalt therapy's sophisticated yet practical theory.

Psychotherapy in This Uncertain Age

"May you live in interesting times." All of us, therapists and clients alike, are certainly living under that ancient Chinese curse. Ecologically, in particular, we are living in an age of unprecedented uncertainty. Our planet, the very ground of our existence, is undergoing profound change, with humanity's future looking anything but certain. Despite living in these "interesting times," however, our clients face all the challenges of shaping lives of love and meaningful work that people have grappled with throughout the ages. Our task as therapists is to help our clients live, fully invested in their lives, while simultaneously supporting them in facing the reality that our collective future is endangered; supporting our clients in fashioning full and forward-looking lives while simultaneously supporting their awareness of the precarious present, presents a paradoxical challenge for psychotherapy in the 21st century.

From both an ecological and a social perspective, we live in a time of growing uncertainty that poses new ethical and clinical challenges for psychotherapy. The gap between rich and poor has become excessive and extreme. Autocratic and nationalistic leaders are ascending in the US and Europe. Weapons of mass destruction proliferate, religiously fueled extremism is on the rise, and as the ecological crisis threatens the world's resources, the conditions that give rise to instability and warped ethnic, religious, and nationalistic ideologies are fueled. Creating a caring, nurturing atmosphere for our clients and working with them in the context of these unsettling environmental, political, and social conditions is a great challenge for modern psychotherapy.

In the spiritual dimension, our clients seek meaning, connection to others, and connection to the greater whole. In our consultation rooms, we psychotherapists do our part to support our clients in their search for connection and meaning in this time of critical social and ecological change. In an age when traditional religions are in decline, the ritual of coming to the psychotherapy group can become quite meaningful in a client's life, offering an environment where vulnerabilities can be shared safely, truths can be spoken, and meaning searched for.

Meanwhile, remarkable changes in our scientifically informed understanding of the nature of reality have shifted our worldview from one of separateness to one of relationality. New understandings in physics inform us that even seemingly inert matter, at the most fundamental level, can be understood as energy in relationship (Capra & Luisi, 2014). Similarly, advances in neuroscience offer new models of the mind that bring us to a fuller appreciation of the fundamental role of relationship and attachment to our cognitive and emotional health (Rifkin, 2009; Wallin, 2007). GGT, in its theory and methodology, is deeply relational, and fits well with the relational or systems view of life that is revolutionizing so much in the sciences and psychology.[2]

Why Gestalt Group Therapy?

Gestalt group therapy has stood the test of time as a deeply wise and resilient approach to understanding the human condition and to promoting growth and fulfillment. As it was originally developed, gestalt therapy was a socially progressive, holistic alternative to conservative trends in psychoanalysis. It turned the primary focus of psychology away from the internal conflicts of the individual and considered the process of making contact between self and other as the starting point for understanding growth and health. First developed in the 1950s by Frederick Perls, MD, his wife Laura Perls, PhD, and the brilliant man of letters, Paul Goodman, PhD, gestalt therapy replaced Freud's instincts and drive model with a humanistic model that embraced growth, choice, and freedom. Assigning the process of contact-making between person and person as the centerpiece of their psychology was a radical choice for gestalt therapy's founders, and it pointed gestalt therapy in the direction of a *relationality* that modern gestaltists have much more fully elaborated (Hycner & Jacobs, 1995; Wheeler, 2013; Yontef, 1993).

Although the theory of gestalt therapy provides an excellent meta-theory for group therapy, gestalt therapy's founders were not focused on group process. The traditional gestalt group method has been for the leader to work with individuals in the group, one at a time, and for group members to provide feedback after the work with the leader. This approach creates a very leader-centered group atmosphere with much individual work happening at great depth, but with insufficient attention paid to group-level issues. This approach has come to be known as the "hot seat" or "open seat" method: the client who is currently working with the leader sitting in the hot or open seat.

The first major publication that began to move gestalt therapy away from the hot seat came in 1980 with Bud Feder and Ruth Ronall's aptly named *Beyond the Hot Seat: Gestalt Approaches to Group*. This collection contained several important chapters that describe working with group dynamics from a gestalt theoretical perspective. A particularly influential chapter from that collection was written by Elaine Kepner, PhD, and provides a phase model for an interactive gestalt group approach. Since that publication, many articles and several books have been written on gestalt therapy from a group process and group dynamics orientation.

As mentioned above, gestalt therapy is a powerful integration of numerous complex systems of thought, including: progressive psychoanalysis, gestalt psychology, field theory, phenomenology, and Martin Buber's philosophy of dialogue. We will discuss each of these in more depth in the coming chapters, particularly in Chapter 1. Gestalt *group* therapy focuses this potent integration on working interactively with groups. GGT's strong theoretical base provides the foundation to work with the many complexities and difficulties we 21st century group therapists face. For example, field theory provides a framework for dealing with a variety of broader issues affecting the life of group members, such as threats to the environment, as well as social and political challenges. Phenomenology helps GGT therapists understand the great diversity of points of view, narratives, and experiences that clients bring to the group experience. Martin Buber's philosophy of dialogue (1992) provides a rich framework for understanding how people can meet one another in the group with empathy and presence. Buber also helps us understand the spiritual dimensions of GGT work—not in a religious sense, but in the sense of appreciating the sacredness of the meeting of people in sharing their vulnerability and their truth. Relational psychoanalysis provides a deep and powerful framework for understanding human development in relational terms. We explore these themes in Chapter 2.

As we will see in the chapters and case examples to come, the capacity for relational living lies at the heart of human growth and development. And this is where GGT really excels. For nowhere is there a more powerful place to explore our relationality than in group. In GGT, group members explore, in-vivo, how we connect with others, how we relate, how we attach, how we protect ourselves, how we deal with excitement, with our hopes and dreams, our disappointments, our shame, our pride, our contempt, our sexuality, our body image, our fears, our emotions, our issues with authority, and a myriad of other issues. The gestalt therapy group becomes a community of people who invest time and trust in one another, becoming known and important to each other, and contributing to each other's growth and development.

Notes

1 Gestalt psychology is separate and distinct from gestalt therapy. Gestalt psychology refers to a school of research psychologists prominent in Germany in the pre-World War II period focusing on a holistic approach to human perception and cognition, whereas gestalt therapy refers to the school of psychotherapy first developed by Frederick and Laura Perls.

2 Fritjof Capra and Pier Luigi Luisi's book, *The Systems View of Life: A Unifying Vision*, is a tour de force examination of the new, relational paradigm. Also excellent in this regard is *The Empathic Civilization* by Jeremy Rifkin.

References

Bocian, B. (2010). *Fritz Perls in Berlin, 1893–1933: Expressionism, psychoanalysis, Judaism*. Bergisch Gladbach, Germany: EHP.

Buber, M. ([1923] 1970). *I and thou* (W. Kaufmann, Trans.). New York: Charles Scribner's Sons.

Buber, M. (1992). *On intersubjectivity and cultural creativity*. Chicago, IL: University of Chicago Press.

Capra, F., & Luisi, P. L. (2014). *The systems view of life: A unifying vision*. Cambridge: Cambridge University Press.

Feder, B., & Ronall, R. (Eds) (1980). *Beyond the hot seat: Gestalt approaches to group*. New York: Brunner/Mazel.

Hycner, R., & Jacobs, L. (1995). *The healing relationship in Gestalt therapy: A dialogic/self psychology approach*. Highland, NY: Gestalt Journal Press.

Kepner, E. (1980). Gestalt group process. In B. Feder & R. Ronall (Eds), *Beyond the hot seat: Gestalt approaches to group* (pp. 5–24). New York: Brunner/Mazel.

Perls, F. S. (1973). *The Gestalt approach and eyewitness to therapy*. New York: Bantam Books.

Perls, F. S., Hefferline, R., & Goodman, P. (1951). *Gestalt therapy: Excitement and growth in the human personality*. New York: Julian Press.

Rifkin, J. (2009). *The empathic civilization: The race to global consciousness in a world in crisis*. New York: Penguin.

Wallin, D. (2007). *Attachment in psychotherapy*. New York: Guilford Press.

Wheeler, G. (2013). *Beyond individualism: Toward a new understanding of self, relationship, and experience*. London: Taylor & Francis.

Yontef, G. M. (1993). *Awareness, dialogue and process: Essays on Gestalt therapy*. Highland, NY: Gestalt Journal Press.

Chapter 1

An Overview of Contemporary Gestalt Therapy for Group Therapists

This chapter is written in Peter's voice

Gestalt therapy can be understood as an integration of socially progressive psychoanalysis, gestalt psychology, Kurt Lewin's field theory, the dialogical existentialism of the philosopher Martin Buber, and existential phenomenology. Gestalt carries a flavor of Zen Buddhism, with its emphasis on awareness and acceptance of "what is." Gestalt therapy has a tradition of being politically progressive, anti-authoritarian, pro-gay rights, feminist, and positive about the creative, consensual expression of human sexuality in its many manifestations. Gestalt therapy appreciates the community while celebrating the individual.

Gestalt's founders, Frederick and Laura Perls, were deeply involved in socially progressive psychoanalysis and gestalt psychology in pre-World War II Germany. They were culturally and politically active in this period, with involvements ranging from those with expressionist theater to socialist political movements (Bocian, 2010). As refugees from fascism, the Perls eventually came to New York, where they were involved in the bohemian culture of Greenwich Village. Social theorist Paul Goodman joined forces with them in New York. In 1951, Frederick Perls and Paul Goodman collaborated, along with Ralph Hefferline, in gestalt therapy's first and most intellectually challenging book: *Gestalt Therapy: Excitement and Growth in the Human Personality* ([1951] 1994). In the 1950s, Frederick and Laura Perls began training therapists in gestalt therapy methodology in New York and beyond.

In the 1960s, Frederick Perls grew his hair and beard long, moved to the West Coast, and spent several years in residence at the Esalen Institute. He became widely known to those who trained with him simply as "Fritz." During this period, Fritz contributed to the sixties counter-culture with his writings, films, and a popularized message of freedom, living in the "here and now," and taking personal responsibility. Fritz achieved fame during the 1960s, but the popularized view of gestalt therapy that he disseminated during this period gave many casual observers an oversimplified view of gestalt therapy. It should be noted that, during the 1960s, when his popular image and sayings seemed to convey an oversimplified "pop psychology" version of gestalt therapy to the public, Fritz and his California-based training partner, Dr. Jim Simkin, nevertheless trained therapists carefully and rigorously (B. Resnick, personal communication, July 25, 2016). Meanwhile, Laura Perls continued to train therapists in New York during the 1960s, and distanced herself from the counter-culture persona that Fritz projected during that period. Since Frederick Perls's death in 1971, gestalt therapy has gone through many changes and permutations.

For our purposes as gestalt *group* therapists, the contributors that have been most influential since Perls's death are:

1. The "relational" school of gestalt therapy; that is, theorists who blend the work of intersubjective psychoanalysis and Martin Buber's dialogical approach into gestalt therapy's already rich integrative framework. Prominent in this current group of contributors are Margherita Spagnuolo Lobb (2014), Lynne Jacobs (1992), Gary Yontef (1993, 2009), and Gordon Wheeler (2013).
2. Philip Lichtenberg (2013), of the Gestalt Therapy Institute of Philadelphia, who emphasizes the unity of self and social.
3. The "Cleveland" school of gestaltists, who have integrated group therapy theory and systems theory with gestalt therapy. Prominent in this group are Isabel Fredericson, Joseph Handlon (1998), Elaine Kepner (1980), Ed Nevis (2013), Sonia Nevis (2003), Erv and Miriam Polster (1974), and Joseph Zinker (1998).
4. Erv Polster (1987), with his emphasis on personal narrative that is so crucial to our group work.
5. Bud Feder, whose books *Beyond the Hot Seat: Gestalt Approaches to Group* (1980) and *Gestalt Group Therapy: A Practical Guide* (2013) have laid invaluable foundations for our current work.

In this chapter I will present a map of gestalt therapy fundamentals with an emphasis on those aspects of the original theory and newer theoretical/methodological developments that will be useful for group therapists. This chapter is written for group therapists who have not previously been exposed to gestalt therapy theory and for gestalt therapists interested in how gestalt theory can serve as a theoretical foundation for group work. It is not comprehensive by any means. I have included some very brief clinical examples to help illustrate the ideas I am presenting. In some cases, I will use group therapy examples to illustrate the ideas, and in others I will use individual therapy examples.

Field Theory

The social psychologist Kurt Lewin developed the concept of *field theory*, which was inspired by Einstein's physics, which revealed the unity of space, time, and gravity. Just as the gravitation of planets can only be understood in relation to the space/time field in which those planets are embedded, people can only be understood in the context of the social world in which we are embedded. Each person lives within a "life-space," which is "the world as perceived by a person relating to it" (Gaffney & O'Neill, 2013, p. 442). Our life-space is that aspect of the field we directly experience. We are not simply influenced by the field, we are *of* the field.

Lewin's field theory places the individual in a social and environmental context. It emphasizes the unity of the personal and the social. Field theory provides a unifying framework from which gestalt therapy conceptualizes our interdependence and interconnectedness. Psychologically, field theory informs individual and group therapy in a number of important ways. It informs us that the individual grows and develops in a context of environmental responsiveness. Conversely, emotional and moral growth will tend to be hindered in an unresponsive, mis-attuned, or abusive environment. Gestalt's field theory orientation suggests that the individual and the society need not be in the kind of fundamental conflict that Sigmund Freud describes in his classic text of conservative psychology, *Civilization and Its Discontents* (1962), whereby society must thwart the individual's destructive and selfish desires for the collective good. Field theory instead sees an individual who can thrive within the ecosystem of his or her social and physical world. In health, the individual's satisfaction will tend to enhance the collective, not detract from it. Gestalt therapy's vision of the field is one in which the individual finds her potential through environmental responsiveness, which then leads to self-support. Far from the conservative aspect of Freud's view that the individual, if unimpeded, will act in her self-interest and against the good of society, the field theory view holds the more optimistic view that when the individual reaches her true potential, she will tend to enhance and enrich her society.

This vision of the field provides an ethical and aesthetic framework for gestalt group therapy (GGT). If the whole group represents a microcosm of the larger field, then each group member's growth depends on the group's responsiveness to the individual. Conversely, the group is enhanced when each group member gets in touch with his or her potential. Field and individual are of the same stuff—each depends on the other for its development. The whole group becomes an increasingly rich environment as its members grow, while each member's growth is enhanced by the richness and complexity of the group as a living system.

Phenomenology

Gestalt therapy theory is a tapestry made up of many theoretical threads, all of which emphasize the humanistic values of respect for the client's experience and a non-pathologizing, accepting approach to psychotherapy. Phenomenology, a concept that derives from the world of existential philosophy, is one of the threads that holds this tapestry together. Phenomenology (Husserl, in Welton, 1999; Spinelli, 2005) is a method that supports the therapist in suspending judgments about the lived experience of both client and therapist. The client's embodied, conscious experience is deeply valued by the gestalt therapist, and the therapist's judgments concerning causality, veracity, or meaning are "bracketed," put aside or accounted for, such that the therapist's attention is directed to *being with* the client in his or her subjective awareness rather than to explaining, changing, or interpreting the client's experience.

The phenomenal field is the "meeting place" wherein the therapist and client make contact, both in their embodied, subjective awarenesses. In the group situation, there is a meeting of all respective group members in their subjectivities. This meeting of group members, each with their own phenomenology, lends a complexity and openness to GGT, which makes for a rich environment for therapist and group members. The therapist stays close to her own phenomenology, attending to her experience of, and responses to, the group. The therapist's basic method is to stay in awareness of her embodied experience of the group. As such, the therapist is open to all that occurs in the group, and avoids interpreting the group's experiences according to any pre-existing template, preferring to be open to the meanings that emerge spontaneously from staying close to the therapist's own and the group members' phenomenal experience.

Gestalt's phenomenological method provides a leavening agent to group therapy's many theories of group phases and group roles (Fairfield, 2004, 2009). Group therapy theorists have written volumes of detailed descriptions of the various phases of group development that may unfold, and various roles that group members might play out in the group (Agazarian, 2004; Beck, 1981). While valuing these theories, gestalt's phenomenological method reminds us to hold these theories lightly.[1] The gestalt group therapist's training is especially challenging in this regard, for the therapist must learn the leading theories of group phases and roles just as any competent group therapist must, and then hold those theories ever so lightly when engaged in group leadership. Informed (but not straitjacketed) by group therapy's theories of group development, the gestalt group therapist bears in mind that the map is not the territory. The therapist is guided by respect for the here-and-now experience of the phenomenal field, mindful that staying with the lived experience of the group will likely yield a richer harvest than relying on preformed theoretical explanations.

The Construction of Our Perceptions

Gestalt therapy takes a constructivist approach to human perception: its view is that health is related to our capacity for constructing orderly, meaningful perceptions of the field. Further, since *self* is fully embedded in the field, the perceptions we construct always include ourselves and point us toward empowered action. This approach to health can be traced to the work of the German neurologist, Kurt Goldstein. In the 1920s, Frederick and Laura Perls (and also the founder of group analysis, S. H. Foulkes) worked in Goldstein's lab in Frankfurt (Bocian, 2010). As the famous neurologist, Oliver Sacks (1995, p. 11), has written about Goldstein's approach to healing:

> *The function of the physician ... is to be as sensitive as possible to all the resonances and ramifications of illness in the individual and so help him to achieve a new organization, an equilibrium. ... One must lead the sick patient through a period of chaos, gently until he can reestablish a new organization, construct[ing] his world anew.*

Goldstein worked with World War I veterans who suffered from brain injuries, helping them through the chaos of neurological damage, working to gently reconstruct their worlds. He studied the human organism as a unified whole. His holism stood in contrast to the popular medical view of his era, which tended to study the parts (organs) as distinct and separate from the whole organism. Goldstein and other gestalt psychologists were greatly interested in issues of perception. They were particularly interested in how it is that people *construct* their perceptions of the world. With those suffering from brain injuries, Goldstein sought to restore their capacity to construct a coherent world of perception and action.

The gestalt psychologists discovered that perception was no passive affair, as had been previously thought (Wheeler, 2013). Old associationist models of perception (Wundt, 1897) gave way to the holistic gestalt view, in which the whole precedes its parts. One of the key understandings from the gestalt psychologists was that human perception is active problem solving and meaning making. The gestalt psychologists explained that when perceiving, for example, a white wooden fence in a field, we perceive first that it is a fence (an object that has human meaning), and then we might proceed to perceive the individual white wooden boards and nails that constitute the parts of the fence (Dreyfuss, 2007). People's perceptions are actively constructed

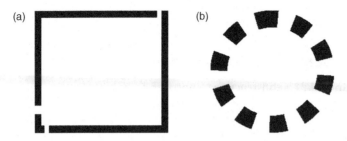

Figure 1.1 Perception of the whole

and follow certain laws of patterning, such that we actively create the perception of whole figures. The pattern of *closure*, for example, is demonstrated in Figure 1.1, where discontinuous lines appear to us first as a box, and only later do we perceive that the box is made up of discontinuous lines. Dots arranged in a circle appear in our minds first as a circle. Only secondarily do we see that what appears to be a circle is made of dots.

Gestalt therapy took the perceptual work of gestalt psychology and applied the constructivist approach to our emotional landscapes and to the meaning we make of our relationships. Our set modes of creatively adjusting become the lens through which we experience our relationships and make meaning of those relationships. One of the key integrations Fritz and Laura Perls made was to bring together the holistic, constructivist, perceptual psychology of gestalt psychology with the revolutionary psychological insights of psychoanalysis. The gestalt therapy that emerged from this integration was something distinct from both of those traditions. Unlike gestalt psychology, gestalt therapy moves far beyond issues of perception and deals with the emotional core of the client's life. Unlike classical Freudian psychology, gestalt therapy concerns itself primarily with how the client is constructing his or her relational and emotional world in the here and now.

In GGT, the constructivist approach is essential to understanding that each member is actively creating his or her perceptions of the group. Group events that barely pass the threshold of consciousness for some group members will be of seminal importance to other group members. Some group members will perceive an emotional tone to the group that is quite distinct from the emotional tone that other group members perceive. Since the gestalt approach presupposes that all group members and leaders are actively constructing their perceptions of the group, there tends to be little point explaining what has "actually" occurred in the group. In a certain sense, each person's perception is true for them since it is they who are constructing their perceptual world.[2]

This understanding has far-reaching consequences for the GGT leader. It puts the leader in the position of "listener" more than that of "explainer" or "interpreter." It increases the leader's fascination with the group, because there is endless and often subtle variation in each group member's perceptual construction of the group experience. It relieves the group leader of the burden of correcting the record. It makes intervening in the group a matter of making contact between differing points of view, rather than interpreting others' experiences.

An example of differing constructions of meaning occurred in one of our training groups. A number of group members shared about lost opportunities in life. One group member's medical studies were irredeemably interrupted by the devastation caused by hurricane Katrina. Another group member grieved the fact that she had let go of a promising career in dance. Another group member's hard-won success in her psychotherapy career had been interrupted by illness. Two distinct points of view seemed to form among group members regarding these losses and accompanying feelings of regret. One subgroup's construction of meaning concerning these regrets was that "it is never too late to go for it," with the basic message being that one should continue to pursue one's original dreams. Others felt that it is best to accept what life gives you and to embrace grief and regrets as an inevitable part of life. As group leaders, there was no need for us to search for the "true" answer to this existential difficulty; our GGT theory supports us in reflecting back to the group the many constructions of meaning and perceptions that are forming in the group, rather than searching for the one true or best construction or narrative.

Creative Adjustments, Fixed Gestalts, Fixed Relational Gestalts, Awareness, and Contact

Perls, Hefferline, and Goodman ([1951] 1994, p. 7) state that, "Psychology is the study of creative adjustments." When the child is met by the parents with mis-attunement to his or her nature and/or needs, the child naturally makes certain creative adjustments in order to cope. For instance, Patricia is a client from a large, prominent, Episcopal family. From the outside, everything looked "perfect," but from the inside Patricia and her siblings were neglected, due to her mother's alcoholism and her father's long hours at the office. A major component of Patricia's creative adjustment in childhood was to keep everything looking perfect on the outside while keeping her inner sense of emotional abandonment and pain well hidden. This was a very adaptive, creative adjustment, given her circumstances in childhood. She played the part of the perfect daughter, and did not rock the boat with her family in order to receive what love and parenting she could. In adulthood, however, the creative adjustments established in childhood—those of hiding her true feelings and putting on a show of perfection—hardened into a fixed gestalt of maintaining a severely perfectionistic veneer over her true feelings of low self-esteem and depression. This split in her led to an eating disorder and depression in early adulthood, which we worked through over many years of individual therapy.

Fixed Gestalts

The creative adjustments we made in childhood (especially those creative adjustments that were established to cope with traumatic circumstances) can become maladaptive in adulthood if and when they are no longer optimally responsive to the situation with which we are currently coping. The old creative adjustments can readily become today's *fixed gestalts*: modes of perception and behavior that function in the background of our awareness, structuring our experience of ourselves and of the world.

For instance, Hal was physically abused in childhood by his father, and made the creative adjustment in childhood of maintaining hyper-alertness. He was always watching for his father's blows, which often came without warning. Hals's creative adjustment was to maintain a hyper-alertness that sometimes helped him avoid attack. However, when Hal came into treatment with me, his hyper-alertness had become habitual and locked in as a fixed gestalt. It had evolved into a timidity that rendered him fearful of other men. In a long-term men's group, Hal experimented with new ways of being with and experiencing other men. He slowly learned to find his voice with other men, to speak his truth, to receive nurturance from them, and let go of his hyper-alertness when in their company.

Fixed Relational Gestalts: Attachment, Excitement, and Shame

The patterns of attunement and mis-attunement at play in our childhood caregiving environment generate a powerful current in each person's life story. Our childhood mode of seeking love within our family of origin creates a template for the attachment style we carry forward in our relationships. Each group member has developed a unique style of attaching. Closely related to this, each group member has his or her style of dealing with excitement and attraction. It can be highly beneficial for the gestalt group therapist to study attachment theory and attachment styles, so that the therapist develops an appreciation of secure, avoidant, ambivalent, and disorganized attachment styles. However, in our discussion of attachment styles, we offer the same caveat that we offer with our discussion of personality styles, group phases, and group roles: *the map is not the territory*. Although the gestalt group therapist must learn current attachment theory, gestalt therapy always holds such theory as a background to and support function for the group members' and leader's phenomenological experience. GGT is an outstanding milieu in which to raise awareness of group members' unique attachment styles, because attaching, along with the themes of attraction, excitement, and love-seeking, are occurring in the here and now of the group process, where we can infuse the experience of these passions with interpersonal connection, awareness, and compassion.

Shame is frequently a mediator of group members' difficulties with excitement, love-seeking, and attachment. This shame is often out of awareness of group members as they connect with each other (Aledort, 2009; Lee, 1996; Wheeler, 2013). We refer to group members' preset patterns of coping with excitement, attraction, and attaching, mediated by unaware shame, as *fixed relational gestalts*. These fixed relational gestalts were formed in the original situation as creative adjustments to a mis-attuned caregiving environment. Group members' fixed relational gestalts will often get enacted in the relationships between group members, and between members and the leader. Because the shame is frequently out of awareness of group members not yet free to express their excitement and needs openly, the growing attachments within the group can become a source of difficulty and a fertile ground for exploration and growth.

Clear and safe sexual boundaries are a vital prerequisite to this manner of exploration. At times, the group member's attractions will be of a primarily sexual nature, while at other times the attraction will be to being held, soothed, comforted, and encouraged. With clarity that group members can explore their attractions in a safe space, where sexual feelings can be expressed but not acted on, it can be very freeing for group members to express attraction to other group members or the group leader who can meet that attraction with openness and understanding.

> Claire is a 30-year-old group member whose father abandoned the family when she was a young child. While loving and devoted, Claire's mother was frequently overwhelmed with making a living, while fighting depression and loneliness. Claire was in long-term gestalt group therapy with Peter and Daisy. We noticed that Claire almost always directed her communication in the group to other group members or to Daisy, but almost never to Peter.

In this excerpt, Claire is talking about going back to school to study for a master's degree in social work:

PETER: Claire—that's my field, and I'm so excited you're considering going into it!

CLAIRE: Thank you, Peter. I didn't know you were interested in me.

PETER: That makes me very sad to hear, Claire—but I'm glad you told me.
    Yes—I *am* very interested in you—excited about your life choices.

CLAIRE: It just seems like you don't reach out to me.

PETER: Okay. Well, I'm glad you let me know that. I sometimes feel something similar—that you don't make eye contact with me, or talk to me much in the group.

CLAIRE: I just don't think I'm the most interesting group member. My life is kind of boring.

PETER: I feel so sad to hear you share this, Claire, but at the same time it feels like a new start for us. I feel very interested in you. I think it's great you're thinking about going back to school, and I love that you're thinking about social work!

CLAIRE: Thanks. I've never gotten much encouragement from men before. It's a new feeling.

PETER: How does it feel, just here and now?

CLAIRE: Good. Scary.

PETER: Okay. I think maybe we're off to a good start. Let's both pay more attention to connecting with each other in group.

CLAIRE: Sounds good.

In this vignette, we see the beginning of working through the shame that mediates Claire's fixed relational gestalt, that she is less interesting to the male leader than are the other group members. This fixed relational gestalt has impeded her ability to receive needed encouragement and mentoring. By making new contact with the leader, the process of creatively adjusting in the relationship begins to take hold, and she begins to unpack the fixed relational gestalt. Over time, Peter and Claire continue this kind of contact, and she takes pleasure in Peter's interest in her development.

Awareness

Any creative adjustment can become a fixed gestalt when there is insufficient support for awareness of the creative adjustment. *Awareness* is the key to working with fixed gestalts, for as long as the fixed gestalt remains out of awareness, it is stuck in place, forever limiting or even distorting our reality. The methodology of GGT is geared to bringing support for awareness of our fixed gestalts, particularly those that show up in our relationships. With this awareness, we learn how to return to the process of *creatively* adjusting, with our perceptions focused on the challenges and opportunities that today's situations present, not the old challenges that we met long ago with the best solutions we could find when we were children.

Awareness of our old, fixed gestalts helps free us from outdated modes of perception, behavior, and adaptation. With the fixed gestalts in awareness, we now have the possibility of choosing new ways of being in the world. Letting go of old, fixed gestalts and embracing new experiences is generally quite challenging for gestalt group members. Change happens primarily through the experience of making contact with other group members in the here and now of the group process. It happens cognitively, emotionally, somatically, and relationally.

Contact

Contact is the fluid and embodied process of fully connecting. We can make contact with other people, with other living things, and even with aspects of ourselves that we have held out of awareness. Usually, however, gestalt therapists use the concept of contact to describe the lived experience of one person connecting with another person. In our relationships, making good quality contact involves our capacity for I–Thou relations with the other, in which we bring our empathy, compassion, and truthfulness. Contact is not just a mental experience; it involves the body as well. This does not mean that contact necessarily involves touch, but it does involve an awareness of our body's response to the other, along with openness to the other's somatic responses to us. Contact involves all of the senses—it is an embodied connection between person and person.

When we are being conscious and present with another person, when we are listening and attending both to ourselves and to the other, then we are making "good quality contact." On the other hand, when we are stuck in our fixed gestalts, and out of the flow of creative adjusting, then we are likely making poor quality contact. The ultimate purpose of GGT is to support its members in making good quality contact through raising awareness of group members' fixed gestalts and through the experience of relating in new and more fulfilling ways.

Figure Formation and the Cycle of Experience

The relationship between *figure* and *ground* is a conceptual framework fundamental to gestalt therapy. *Figure* is what is in the foreground of our experience. *Ground* is what is in the background. At any moment, there are an infinitude of experiences on which one could conceivably focus. Let me write down my experience in this moment as an example of the many things that potentially could become figural for me here and now:

> At the moment I am writing this, I am sitting on a plane, heading to a conference. I am listening to Beethoven's Ninth Symphony on my headphones. From time to time I am stirred by the music, and I could choose to close my eyes and let Beethoven become fully figural. Daisy, my wife (and co-author), is sitting to my left and having trouble with her iPhone. I take a moment to help her out, and I feel a hint of certain emotional themes in our relationship that could

come into a bright figure with a deep discussion between us. There is a young man and a young woman in the seats in front of us, of seemingly different races, who are striking up a lively conversation. I wonder if a new love is brewing! Their conversation appears sweet and I find myself wondering about who they are and if they will fall in love!

Despite the fact that these possibilities (and countless more) are present in this moment, I am focused on writing these words. It is my writing which is *figural* for me in this moment. The other events remain in the *background* of my awareness. In gestalt therapy, this relationship between figure and ground is vital. Figure and ground apply to our emotional lives, as well as to our perceptions. For example:

> A few days ago, my cousin died after a long battle with cancer. I feel very sad about losing her and, if I feel into that sadness, it can readily become figural for me. Also in the background is the excitement I feel about some very positive developments in my daughter's life. Additionally, in my background are family-of-origin issues that I've been working on lately in my own psychotherapy, which bring up very complicated feelings of grief and anxiety.

All of these emotional undercurrents can and do emerge into my foreground when I receive sufficient support for them from others and give them enough self-support. Yet what feels figural for me in this moment is the experience of this writing; the feeling driving me is a desire to communicate to you, the reader, these ideas, which have been so powerfully helpful to me, and which I hope will help you better understand your work as a group therapist.

The Cycle of Experience and the Significance of Action

What emerges from the background of our consciousness, and becomes figural for us, usually relates to what we *need*. An obvious example of this is that the smell of food being cooked will become highly figural for a hungry person, whereas it may remain unnoticed and in the background of the consciousness of one who is satiated. A more subtle example of this is that, when I am in need of grieving the death of a loved one, a sad James Taylor song playing softly in the background suddenly sounds compelling and beautiful to me—it becomes *figural*. The song points me to the need of attending to the unfinished business of grieving the death of a loved one.

Dr. Joseph Zinker (1977, 1998) introduced the *cycle of experience* to map the healthy flow between what becomes figural for us and the action we take in the world. I have changed Zinker's wording and concepts here slightly:

Sensation → Awareness → Mobilization of energy → Contact → New equilibrium

Let us illustrate with a group leadership example:

Sensation—Daisy and I are leading a group, and I'm feeling annoyed with Tony, a group member who seems to be continually correcting me when I speak in group. I *sense* a rush of anger/adrenaline when he interrupts me, and I notice that I talk over him.

Awareness → Mobilization of energy—A conflict is forming between Tony and me. As I sit with the feeling, I begin to become *aware* that something in our relationship is getting enacted in the group, but I'm not sure what. I *mobilize* myself to take the situation to my peer consultation group, and with their support I gain new awareness and insight into what is going on between Tony and me. With my consultation group, I explore the anger I feel when my authority in the group is challenged. They help me get underneath my anger to my vulnerability, and an old gestalt of not being seen by my father as smart enough, and not being mentored by my father into manhood. This can trigger in me a need for authority and control in which I do not like to be challenged, particularly when I am in a leadership role. I also gain insight into issues that might be triggering Tony in the group, particularly the feeling that his father was ineffectual and weak, which made Tony quite anxious and angry at his father.

Contact—In the next group, when I experience Tony interrupting me, I am able to meet him *contactfully*. I do not feel angry or threatened, because I have been able to bring the old gestalts into awareness, and now I welcome the opportunity to talk with Tony about what this brings up for me, while inviting him to explore with me what is going on between us and within himself. Out of this contact evolves a deeply involving piece of work.

New equilibrium—Now Tony, the group, and I all have had a new experience, one from which we all have grown. The old figure—that of Tony and me getting into conflict—is resolved for now. We have a *new equilibrium*. From this new place, new figures will form, leading to new action and new contact.

The cycle of experience flows from gestalt therapy's field orientation. The cycle of experience is a working model for understanding how the individual, within the context of the field, creatively adjusts to the self-in-field situation through awareness and contactful action. It is a model of self-empowerment as well as a model of social action, for gestalt's roots in progressive psychoanalysis emphasize self–social unity rather than self–social disparity (Lichtenberg, 2013). In health, the individual who actualizes his or her own potential will be adding to the overall richness of the field.

As a gestalt group leader, the cycle of experience can serve as an intervention model, as discussed above in the example with Tony, and as a model of empowerment for group members. We teach group members that their responses to the situations in their lives provide them with invaluable information as to how to proceed with getting their needs met. A quick example of this is Taylor, who in group talked about needing time with her dad, but feeling very put off by her jealous stepmother. The *sensation* of feeling solid and strong when she has contact with her dad led to an *awareness* that she needs more time with him, but has been put off by her stepmother. Taylor *mobilized her energy* and overcame her resistance to reaching out to him. This led to new *contact* with her dad in which she asserted with him her need for more time. They worked out an arrangement for bi-weekly meetings at a coffee shop, apart from the stepmother. Taylor, her dad, and her stepmother reached a *new equilibrium* in which Taylor's needs were better attended to.

Boundaries and Boundary Disturbances

In the above example, we see how Taylor needed to recalibrate the boundaries in her relationships with both her father and her stepmother. She needed to be closer to her father and to have more distance from her stepmother. Healthy boundaries are essential to our clients' well-being. In understanding gestalt therapy's approach to boundaries, we come back to gestalt's field orientation. We individuals are embedded in the field. We are creatures of the field. Yet, at the same time, we exist within defined boundaries. If we simply existed within an undifferentiated field, we would cease to exist as individuals, and, in a certain way, without boundaries we would cease to exist at all.

Think of the boundaries that a mother maintains for her infant. She protects her infant from the elements with her own body and her care. Without the protective boundaries she provides, the child would surely die. Without that protective boundary, if the field were undifferentiated, no child could thrive.

So, how does gestalt therapy map the territory of boundaries in good health and the disturbances to boundaries in ill health? How is our existence within the field differentiated so that we can thrive in our life-space?

Our boundaries can be broadly understood to form in three distinct styles:

1   Confluence
2   Isolation
3   Contact

Confluence refers to boundaries that are undifferentiated. As two rivers become one at the point of their confluence, so it is that people can become so enmeshed as to lose their individual identity. Confluence becomes problematic when, out of awareness, we merge with the other and lose our own perspective. A classic example of confluence is the codependent spouse of an alcoholic, who has lost his or her own perspective on the spouse's addiction.

Isolation refers to the condition in which there is little or no connection between people. Isolation describes a state of alienation and disconnection. Isolation becomes problematic when we need the stimulation and nurturance that interpersonal connection may offer, but we lack the support to seek that connection. An example of isolation was a very successful executive who was diagnosed with cancer and had to leave his job. Unskilled at reaching out for support, he became highly isolated.

Contact is the boundary style that connotes a healthy balance between connection and autonomy. In contact, there is a flow with which we can shuttle between our inner world and the interpersonal world. The executive mentioned above had typically made contact with others from a vantage point of power, strength, and authority. His cancer and loss of career took away these supports for making contact. In group, he had to learn how to make contact with a new set of supports, utilizing his vulnerability and humanity to make contact with others. Learning to do so was deeply enriching for him.

Projection is the boundary disturbance of seeing in the other what has not yet been integrated into the self. In GGT, we encounter projection frequently. Projection is frequently at play when one group member has a particularly strong reaction to another group member. For instance, in one of our groups, Mary developed a strong dislike for Ellen. Mary found Ellen to be far too entitled to group time and group support. When Mary encountered Ellen's sometimes insensitive demands on group time, Mary projected strongly negative feelings onto Ellen and judged Ellen's use of group time to be highly inappropriate. Meanwhile, other group members tended to get mildly annoyed when Ellen took too much time, but for them it was not a big deal.

In time, it became clear that Mary was unable to reach out for the support that she so deeply needed. Mary needed more group time and the self-support to ask for it. When Ellen took group time, it triggered old feelings derived from Mary's family, in which Mary's parents attended to her sister and ignored Mary. Mary was projecting her sibling anger onto Ellen, as well as her disowned desire to receive more attention from the group. Unpacking and owning projections in group can be powerful for the one who is projecting, the one who is being projected upon, and those witnessing the process of re-owning the projected feelings. Mary slowly made progress in re-owning her projections onto Ellen. Concurrently, she worked on reaching out for more group time. In GGT, when group members own their projections, they are integrating those aspects of themselves that had been disowned and projected out onto other group members.

Retroflection

Retroflection occurs when we turn our aggression in on ourselves. In the film *Manhattan* (1979), Woody Allen's character muses: "I can't express anger. … I just grow a tumor instead." Now that is retroflection! Retroflection might be present when group members display depression, low self-esteem, passivity, or passive-aggressive behavior. With retroflection, the energy that in health might energize action to change a bad situation gets turned against the self. The anger takes a U-turn. The classic case of retroflection is the abuse victim, who turns the rage at their abuser into self-hate, while continuing to tolerate the abuse. Undoing retroflected anger can be a liberating and powerful process to witness in gestalt group therapy. It can be thrilling for group members to witness a fellow group member free themselves from the shackles of self-hate and find new empowerment.

Charlie was married to a woman who was drinking heavily and being verbally abusive when intoxicated. His self-esteem was low and he was depressed. Group members confronted his retroflected anger when it showed up in the group interactions, and also encouraged him to set limits with his wife when she was mean to him. Over the course of years, Charlie began to speak up for himself more fully in group and eventually he learned to set better limits on his wife's abusive behavior.

Dialogue

The philosopher Martin Buber was Laura Perls's teacher in pre-World War II Frankfurt. She said of Buber that "he had more influence on me than any other psychologist or psychoanalyst."[3] Laura was deeply impressed by the way Buber "respected people." Buber's influence on gestalt therapy centers on his approach to *dialogue*, and his model of I–Thou/I–It inter-human relations. Below we explore various aspects of Buber's dialogue that are especially salient for GGT (Hycner, 1993; Yontef, 1993).

I–Thou/I–It

For Buber ([1923] 1970, p. 72), "all life is encounter." When we encounter another person from the inclusive position of I–Thou, we open ourselves to the depth of both ourselves and of the other whom we are meeting. When holding the basic position of I–Thou, we encounter others whose subjective experience, including their pleasure, pain, consciousness, somatic, aesthetic, and spiritual experience, is as real as our own.

The basic position of I–It refers to staying on the surface with people. It means viewing others as objects rather than as people with their own lived experience of the world. The basic word *It* objectifies the other and his or her world. This position represents a kind of encounter with the world that *uses* the other rather than *being with* the other.[4] Buber's concept of I–Thou and I–It, which he first published in 1923, has had a profound impact on gestalt therapy. GGT's I–Thou stance points the therapist toward a respectful, inclusive approach. It points to a level, egalitarian relationship between therapist and group members. I–Thou points to the valuing of diversity. It points to a therapy that values the dignity of each group member's experience and phenomenology. GGT is an ideal environment for group members to learn about their inter-human I–Thou and I–It relations, for in GGT, group members have the opportunity to experiment with their relationships, to explore, and to give and receive feedback.

The Between

Buber (1992, p. 39) states:

> The "between" is to be acquired by no longer localizing the relation between human beings, as is customary, either within individual souls or in a general world which embraces and determines them, but in actual fact between them. "Between" is not an auxiliary construction, but the real place and bearer of what happens between men.

Therapist and client may enter the *between* when the therapist dedicates herself to meeting the client as a distinctive individual, bracketing the therapist's presuppositions about who the client *is*, based on categories of diagnosis, gender, ethnicity, group roles, etc. Therapist and client meet on the "narrow ridge," where one utterly unique human being meets another. The individual who is in the therapist's chair is meeting the individual who is in the client's chair, with all the history and systems of meaning with which both therapist and client imbue the experience. Therapist and client meet, and this meeting takes on its own unique character. In the group situation, the meeting of all group members in their individuality gives each group a flavor all its own—one that can never be repeated, and one that has its own unique potential and challenges.

Inclusion, Confirmation, and Presence

Inclusion is the stance of fully taking in the other, while *confirmation* is the act of communicating this to one's partner in the dialogue, and thereby deeply affirming them.

Buber (1992, p. 78) expresses this poetically:

> *The experiencing senses and the imagining of the real which completes the findings of the senses work together to make the other present as a whole and as a unique being as the person that he is. But the speaker does not merely perceive the one who is present to him in this way; he perceives him as his partner, and that means that he confirms this other being, so far as it is for him to confirm.*

Presence is the stance of bringing one's own self and one's own truth to the dialogue. With presence, one is willing to take the risk of bringing forth one's own true thoughts and feelings that arise in the here and now of the dialogue. Again, Buber's own poetic words express it best:

> *[I]f genuine dialogue is to arise, everyone who takes part in it must bring himself into it. And that also means that he must be willing on each occasion to say what is really in his mind about the subject of the conversation. And that means further that on each occasion he makes the contribution of his spirit without reduction and without shifting his ground.*

> (ibid)

Presence does not, however, give one license to say anything at all. Buber beautifully describes the mindfulness required to reach inside for one's truth, and then to bring one's truth forward into speech in such a way as to affirm the other and the ongoing dialogue:

Everything depends on the legitimacy of "what I have to say". And of course I must also be intent to raise into an inner word and then into a spoken word what I have to say at this moment but do not yet possess as speech. To speak is both nature and work, something that grows and something that is made, and where it appears dialogically, in the climate of great faithfulness, it has to fulfill ever anew the unity of the two.

(p. 79)

Stewardship of the Dialogue

There are two aspects to the gestalt therapist's *stewardship of the dialogue* (Hycner, 1993): sustaining the dialogical outlook and commitment to the dialogue:

1. *Sustaining the dialogical outlook*—The gestalt therapist must often hold a dialogical attitude even if the client has no idea of, or capacity for, "Buberian" dialogue. In practice, the client need have no concept of "dialogue" in order for the therapist to assume a dialogical attitude. Sustaining the dialogical outlook, however, can be challenging when the therapist's defenses are triggered.

2. *Commitment to the dialogue* (Yontef, 1993)—The gestalt therapist will generally value contact and the dialogue itself over any agenda she may have for the client. The experience of being in dialogue is as much a healing factor for the client as any advice the therapist may wish to share, and the therapist's attachment to her agenda can work against the dialogical attitude. When the therapist lets the dialogue unfold, she is placing her confidence in the healing power of dialogue to bring forth the issues that require attention.

We will let Martin Buber (1992, p. 79) have the last word on the subject of dialogue:

Where the dialogue is fulfilled in its being, between partners who have turned to one another in truth, who express themselves without reserve and are free of the desire for semblance, there is brought into being a memorable common fruitfulness which is to be found nowhere else. ... The interhuman opens out what otherwise remains unopen.

Embodiment

To engage in dialogue is to be in an embodied I–Thou connection with another. It is a full turning toward the other, not just with our minds and hearts, but with our bodies as well. When I am in the presence of other people, much of what I know about them has very little to do with any words that are said by them or thought by me. Much of what I know, I know from sensing my body's responses. How does this person make me feel? Do I feel expansive when with him? Do I feel contracted? What happens in my heart? What happens in my genitals and in my sexual response? Do I feel heavy or light with him? Do I feel like running away, claustrophobic, or engulfed? Do I feel an angry pounding in my chest around him? Do I feel small and insignificant? Do I feel tired? Alive? Dead? Our body sensations are speaking to us whenever we are in contact with another person. These sensations are a key ingredient of our contact-making and of our capacity for dialogue.

Gestalt therapy supports us in being aware of what our bodies are telling us about self and other. Awareness of the body is essential to gestalt therapy's holism, for it is a fundamental precept of gestalt therapy that we seek to heal the split between mind and body. Our body awareness contributes as much to our intelligence as does our intellectual learning. The body tells us much about what and who we are attracted to, about who we need, and what we want. Our bodies inform us about ourselves, about others, and about the situations we face.

Every Person's Life is Worth a Novel

Gestalt therapy has a great appreciation for each client's history, their stories, and the narratives of their life. Gestalt therapist Erv Polster borrowed French novelist Gustave Flaubert's phrase, "Every person's life is worth a novel," for the title of his lovely book describing the many ways in which gestalt therapy works with our clients' stories. Having trained with Fritz Perls for many years, Polster discusses how Perls "was a master at leading people into reenactments of early life experiences, so vividly restored as to feel almost like a trip in a time capsule" (Polster, 1987, p. 172). Polster explains that both the "here and now" and the client's history are valued in the gestalt approach. The energy and flow of life belong to the here and now, while context and meaning derive from our histories and narratives.

We make contact in the here and now, while the fixed relational gestalts that we bring to that contact are inextricably linked to our history. In GGT we join lives when we share our narratives, our secrets, our large and small stories (Polster, 1987). Group members come to know the important people in each other's lives, not literally, but as the people who populate the narratives of each other's lives. Group members' narratives interconnect and interweave as group members come to know and internalize each other's stories. Stories become a source of connection and empathy between group members. Stories also lend a sense to each group member that they are not alone, because there is so much that connects us in our common human condition.

Of course, when we are remembering and telling a story, the remembering and telling is occurring in the here and now, even though the events we are remembering occurred in the past. The remembering is now occurring within the therapeutic dialogue, which opens up many possibilities for integration, healing, and the letting go of old, fixed gestalts. For instance:

> A group member tells a story about her history of feeling seen by her father only when she was beautiful and exceptional. One thing leads to another and, in the here and now, she has the awareness that she always wears her contact lenses to group rather than her glasses, even though her glasses are often more comfortable to wear. This, she is now aware, is a here-and-now repetition of her fixed gestalt that she will only be loved when she is at her most beautiful. Group members offer encouragement that she experiment with wearing her glasses, which she did the following week, much to the delight of group members, who helped her experience a whole new gestalt—that of being loved and accepted for who she really is, and not for her perfection.

The Paradoxical Theory of Change

We close this chapter with the *paradoxical theory of change*, a simple but powerful idea that can be stated thus: real, lasting change can best occur when we deeply and fully accept "what is." Self-acceptance and a realistic assessment of the current situation are cornerstones of the paradoxical theory of change. Self-acceptance means that I attend to my current positions and feelings without judging myself, even when I dislike or disapprove of my own feelings. Furthermore, it means that I do my best to fully perceive my current situation in its fullest complexity, with all of its opportunities, impediments, difficulties, and possibilities. It is not primarily through force of will that real, lasting change occurs (although our assertion of will certainly is involved). Instead, it is the releasing of our fixed gestalts, our stuck places, that allows us to return to the flow of life. The energy that powers change is already present, for life itself is dynamic. Life is a river with strong currents that can provide the energy for the change we seek. The way to lasting change is not to push the river, but to enter into its flow. Then change becomes much more a matter of steering our boat on the big river of life, rather than pushing the river (Stevens, 1970).

The psychiatrist who first developed gestalt therapy's paradoxical theory of change was Dr. Arnold Beisser. Beisser was a tennis pro and surgeon who was afflicted with polio in his thirties. A highly physical and athletic man, he became paralyzed and needed an iron lung simply to breathe. Beisser re-trained in psychiatry and became a leading psychiatrist in the state of California's mental health system. Beisser developed a close relationship with Fritz Perls when he brought Fritz into a state psychiatric hospital to run training sessions with the staff. Beisser wrote movingly of his friendship with Perls, and it was for Perls's festschrift (R. Resnick, personal communication, July 20, 2016) that Beisser wrote his paper developing the paradoxical theory of change. Gestalt therapist Liv Estrup (2010) has made an engaging and moving film about Beisser's life entitled *Flying Without Wings: Life with Arnold Beisser* (2010).

It is instructive to contemplate the relationship between Beisser's paralysis and the development of his theory. The only way for Beisser to come to terms with his changed status from athlete to quadriplegic was to start with a thoroughgoing acceptance of "what is." His new limitations, his emotional reactions to his losses, the challenges of coping with unrelenting pain and discomfort, loss of mobility, and loss of autonomy all presented extreme challenges. By staying with his experiences of "what is," he opened up the possibility of reconnecting with the flow of life. He found that when he concentrated on something that engaged him, he could temporarily forget his physical discomfort. During his many years of paralysis, Beisser developed an important psychiatric career, positively influenced the lives of many patients, students, and colleagues, wrote a number of inspiring books, and developed a strong, loving, intimate relationship. His paradoxical theory of change was the philosophy by which he was able to live so fully in the face of such extreme limitations—he learned to accept himself and his situation. This acceptance allowed him to connect with the possibilities still present in his life, and to adjust creatively to his environment, maximizing the possibilities both for his own fulfillment and for making many positive contributions in the world.

In an open letter to Fritz Perls, Beisser (1991, p. 126) wrote:

> *Thank you, Fritz, for all you did for me. You were a friend who came into my life at just the right time. I learned so much from you. Although you congratulate me on my change paper, I could not have conceived it except as a result of my work with you. You helped me to make new sense of my disability. You helped me to trust in what may come, and to understand that, no matter what occurs, I always will have some choices open to me.*

Notes

1 We particularly value the phases and roles of group therapy as described by Ariadne Beck, whose work we have found enormously helpful. We thank Jim Fishman, LCSW, for all that he has taught us about Beck's work.

2 Of course, we do not mean this in an extreme sense. A psychotic or pathologi-
cally paranoid group member will certainly suffer from distorted perceptions.
But within more "normal" parameters, it could be perfectly valid for example
that one member experiences the group as loving and supportive while another
member experiences it as competitive and invalidating.

3 www.gestalt.org/laura.htm.

4 Gestalt therapy recognizes that I–It relations are an essential dimension of
human functioning. Additionally, I–Thou moments of meeting involve mutuality and grace that cannot be so much aimed at as prepared for through openness to, and respect for, the other.

References

Agazarian, Y. (2004). *Systems-centered therapy for groups*. London: Karnac
Books.

Aledort, S. (2009). Excitement: A crucial marker for group psychotherapy.
Group, 33(1), 45–62.

Beck, A. P. (1981). Developmental characteristics of the system-forming process.
In J. E. Durkin (Ed.), *Living groups: Group psychotherapy and general system
theory*. New York: Brunner/Mazel.

Beisser, A. R. (1971). Paradoxical theory of change. In J. Fagan & I. L. Shepherd
(Eds), *Gestalt therapy now* (pp. 77–80). New York: Harper Colophon.

Beisser, A. R. (1991). *The only gift*. New York: Doubleday.

Bocian, B. (2010). *Fritz Perls in Berlin, 1893–1933: Expressionism, psychoanalysis, Judaism*. Bergisch Gladbach, Germany: EHP.

Buber, M. ([1923] 1970). *I and thou* (W. Kaufmann, Trans.). New York: Charles
Scribner's Sons.

Buber, M. (1992). *On intersubjectivity and cultural creativity*. Chicago, IL:
University of Chicago Press.

Dreyfuss, H. (2007) Heidegger. Retrieved from https://archive.org/details/
Philosophy_185_Fall_2007_UC_Berkeley.

Estrup, L. (Producer and Director). (2010). *Flying Without Wings: Life with
Arnold Beisser* [Motion picture]. Available from livestrup.com

Fairfield, M. (2004). Gestalt groups revisited: A phenomenological approach.
Gestalt Review, 8(3), 336–357.

Fairfield, M. (2009). Dialogue in complex systems: The hermeneutical attitude.
In L. Jacobs & R. Hycner (Eds), *Relational approaches in gestalt therapy* (pp.
193–220). Santa Cruz, CA: Gestalt Press.

Feder, B. (1980). *Beyond the hot seat: Gestalt approaches to group*. New York:
Brunner/Mazel.

Feder, B. (2006). *Gestalt group therapy: A practical guide*. New Orleans, LA:
Gestalt Institute Press.

Feder, B. (2013). *Gestalt group therapy: A practical guide*. Illawara, Australia:
Ravenwood Press.

Freud, S., & Sigmund Freud Collection (Library of Congress). (1962). *Civilization
and its discontents*. New York: W.W. Norton.

Gaffney, S., & O'Neill, B. (2013). *The gestalt field perspective: Methodology and
practice*. Illawara, Australia: Ravenwood Press.

Handlon, J. H., & Fredericson, I. (1998). What changes the individual in Gestalt groups? A proposed theoretical model. *Gestalt Review, 2*, 275–294.

Hycner, R. (1993). *Between person and person: Toward a dialogical psychotherapy*, 2nd edition. Highland, NY: Gestalt Journal Press.

Jacobs, L. (1992). Insights from psychoanalytic self psychology and intersubjectivity theory for gestalt therapists. *Gestalt Journal, 15*(2), 25–60.

Kepner, E. (1980). Gestalt group process. In *Beyond the hot seat: Gestalt approaches to group* (pp. 5–24). New York: Brunner/Mazel.

Lee, R. G. (1996). Shame and the Gestalt model. In *The voice of shame: Silence and connection in psychotherapy* (pp. 3–21). New York: Routledge.

Lichtenberg, P. (2013). *Community and confluence: Undoing the clinch of oppression*. New York: Taylor & Francis.

Lobb, M. S. (2014). *The now-for-next in psychotherapy: Gestalt therapy recounted in post-modern society*. Siracusa, Italy: Istituto di Gestalt HCC Italy.

Nevis, E. C. (2013). *Organizational consulting: A Gestalt approach*. New York: Taylor & Francis.

Nevis, S., Backman, S., & Nevis, E. C. (2003). Connecting strategic and intimate interactions: The need for balance. *Gestalt Review, 7*(2), 134–146.

Perls, F., Hefferline, R., & Goodman, P. ([1951] 1994). *Gestalt therapy: Excitement and growth in the human personality*. New York: Gestalt Journal Press.

Polster, E. (1987). *Every person's life is worth a novel*. New York: W. W. Norton & Co.

Polster, E. (1995). *A population of selves: A therapeutic exploration of personal diversity*. San Francisco, CA: Jossey-Bass.

Polster, E., & Polster, M. (1974). *Gestalt therapy integrated*. New York: Vintage.

Sacks, O. (1995). Foreword. In K. Goldstein, *The organism* (pp. 7–14). New York: Zone Books.

Spinelli, E. (2005). *The interpreted world: An introduction to phenomenological psychology*. London: Sage.

Stevens, B. (1970). *Don't push the river (it flows by itself)*. Boulder, CO: Real People Press.

Welton, D. (Ed.) (1999). *The essential Husserl: Basic writings in transcendental phenomenology*. Bloomington, IN: Indiana University Press.

Wheeler, G. (2013). *Gestalt reconsidered: A new approach to contact and resistance*. New York: Taylor & Francis.

Wundt, W. M. (1897). *Outlines of psychology*. New York: W. Engelmann.

Yontef, G. (1993). *Awareness, dialogue and process: Essays on gestalt therapy*. Highland, NY: Gestalt Journal Press.

Yontef, G. (2009). The relational attitude in gestalt theory and practice. In L. Jacobs & R. Hycner (Eds), *The relational approach in gestalt therapy* (pp. 37–59). New York: GestaltPress/Routledge.

Zinker, J. (1977). *Creative process in gestalt therapy*. New York: Brunner/Mazel.

Zinker, J. (1998). *In search of good form: Gestalt therapy with couples and families*. New York: Taylor & Francis.

Chapter 2

Relational Development in Gestalt Group Therapy

This chapter is written in the voices of both Peter and Daisy

In this chapter,[1,2] we will present some of the themes, modes of thinking, and methods that have emerged in our pursuit of a gestalt group therapy model that promotes relational development. We define *relational development* as a growing capacity for creative, empowered living that is deeply connected to self and other. Our therapeutic approach to advancing relational development in GGT involves the promotion of growth for each individual group member, and for the group itself as an increasingly humane and facilitative environment. Our model has evolved into a weaving together of three threads: the first two are developmental threads involving individual group members; the third involves working with the group-as-a-whole. These three threads are:

- A classical gestalt therapy view of growth, which places emphasis on awareness, authenticity, agency, healthy boundaries, experimentation, self-support, and choice. We refer to this thread as the *self-activating* aspect of relational development (Perls, 1973; Resnick, 1978; Simkin, 1998).
- A contemporary/relational gestalt therapy view of growth, which places an emphasis on empathy, connection, dialogue, and sensitivity to the vulnerabilities that accompany relationality. We will refer to this thread as the *intimately connected* aspect of relational development (Jacobs & Hycner, 1995; Staemmler, 2009; Wheeler, 2000; Yontef, 1993).
- A field-oriented view of group development, which integrates the principles of group process and group dynamics. From this perspective, the group is seen as a facilitating environment for each group member's growth and development. We will refer to this thread as the *group-as-a-whole* aspect of gestalt group development (Aylward, 1996; Fairfield, 2009; Feder, 2006; Kepner, 1980).

In weaving together these threads, new modes of thinking about GGT have arisen for us—modes that have emerged from our earlier training and experiences, but that cannot be traced back linearly to what we have previously learned, because these new models are the products of emergent processes that were forged in the crucible of many years' absorption in leading, studying, and participating in gestalt and psychodynamic groups. The purpose of this chapter is to articulate these new ways of thinking, intervening, and working in gestalt groups. The organizing idea underlying all of the musings, reflections, and case examples in this chapter is simply stated: the gestalt group can be felicitously approached as a microcosm of the group member's relational universe, and working creatively with the group process provides abundant opportunities for the growth and development of each member's capacity for relational development.

Our Journey with Gestalt Groups: Some Personal Background

We have been co-leading gestalt therapy treatment, growth, and training groups for over 20 years. For the first 10 years or so, we practiced GGT in the modality we had been taught by our gestalt mentors, working primarily within a model that focuses on individual pieces of work within the group. We did much meaningful work in this mode, and still frequently do individual pieces of work in the group. Over time, however, we began to notice issues, dilemmas, and complications developing in the background of the group experience, issues that felt underdeveloped in our group work. Such issues included group-as-a-whole phenomena, such as conflicts or ruptures occurring within our groups, group members feeling excluded, group members feeling hurt or damaged by the group experience, and unexpressed eroticism and competition. Furthermore, there were many bad feelings that *we* carried away from the group experience, as the unexpressed material affected us as well as the group members.

Reading Bud Feder and Ruth Ronall's seminal collection, *Beyond the Hot Seat: Gestalt Approaches to Group* (1980), gave us new ways of thinking about gestalt groups and provided us with models of understanding group process and group development. We resonated with Feder and Ronall's statement (p. xii):

> [T]he group-as-a-whole—more than and different from the sum of its parts—is a powerful force for better or worse. If recognized and skillfully used by the leader, the forces inherent in the group become agents for growth and healing; if ignored, misunderstood or misused, these forces can prevent or hamper growth and movement, and their effect can be toxic.

Beyond the Hot Seat convinced us that we needed to pursue further training. Reading about these new, more interactive approaches to working with gestalt groups piqued our interest, yet we lacked the skills necessary to work in a highly interactive, process-oriented mode. We felt that fundamental gestalt understandings, such as the paradoxical theory of change, commitment to the dialogue, the promotion of awareness, and field theory, could be thoroughly applicable in a context that seeks to develop the group-as-a-whole along with the individuals in the group.

A terrible event provided further motivation to our search for new skills in leading gestalt groups. A beloved gestalt trainer, a man who had been a major mentor for me (Peter) in the hot-seat model and had been my therapist for many years, committed suicide one night immediately after leading a gestalt therapy training group. This tragic and traumatic event underscored for us the importance of pursuing further understanding of the powerful forces at work in gestalt therapy groups—forces that impact group members and leaders alike.

This search led us to the Washington School of Psychiatry's National Group Psychotherapy Institute. At the Washington School we learned to better understand groups as systems and to think more deeply about the role of the leader in fostering individual and group development. We learned how and why to work with group-as-a-whole perspectives, about stereotypical group roles that can form and get acted out in harmful ways, about how to address issues working powerfully in the group background, such as competition and eroticism, and about new ways to understand group dynamics.

We have journeyed on the path of both gestalt group membership and gestalt group leadership for many years now. This chapter is a reflection on the models we have developed on this journey of learning and practice; it reflects ways of thinking about GGT that animate our current work.

A Relational Approach to the Self in Gestalt Group Therapy

As we discussed in Chapter 1, gestalt therapy proposes that the *self* can be best conceptualized as the active process of living at the contact boundary where the individual meets the environment. The *self* that occurs at the contact boundary is always developing, changing, and in process. Gestalt therapy's understanding of the self emphasizes fluidity and emergent processes rather than cemented certainty. When we speak of the environment, we are referring to other people, to the physical, natural, and social environments within which we individuals exist. The environment, too, is always fluid, evolving, and dynamic.

Perls, Hefferline, and Goodman (1951, p. 235) refer to the *self* as "the system of contacts at any moment ... the self is the contact-boundary at work." It is sometimes said in gestalt therapy that "self is a verb." This active and process-oriented approach to the self provides for a particularly good fit with a process-oriented approach to group therapy. In GGT, where contacting is a two-way street, the group process provides many opportunities to work with the person who initiates contact and with the other, also present in the group, who receives the contact and in turn has his or her own subjective experience of the contact. When the process of contacting occurs within a group container that values awareness, growth, empathy, and truthfulness, then the conditions are ripe for a relationally rich path to emotional growth. This emotional growth is infused with a growing capacity to stay connected with all things human in self and other. We refer to this emotional growth, cultivated in the interactive connectedness of gestalt group therapy, as *relational development*.

Two Aspects of Relational Development: The Self-Activating Aspect and the Intimately Connected Aspect

We have identified two distinct threads that are woven together to create the tapestry of relational development: the *self-activating aspect* and the *intimately connected aspect*. Let us look at each in turn.

The classical or Perlsian (referring to Fritz Perls) thread in gestalt therapy, which we will refer to as the *self-activating* aspect, pursues the sensibility of a self, occurring at the contact boundary with sufficient aggression and sense of agency to de-structure the introjected givens, to find and assert one's voice, and to forge a full, authentic, and well-lived life. An important metaphor in this mode is the act of chewing—the act of chewing means that we do not swallow our food whole. Psychologically, by "chewing" we de-structure the "shoulds" that we have introjected and learn to live with authenticity and choice. For example, a vital ingredient of the Perlsian thread is gestalt therapy's historical acceptance of same-sex attraction and refusal to pathologize homosexual needs and desires. The self-activating aspect searches for authenticity, not for conformity to societal, familial, or classical Freudian prejudices. The aesthetic of the self-activating aspect reflects strength, clarity, and authenticity.

The contemporary thread in gestalt therapy focuses on empathy and the interpersonal qualities that we bring to the boundary in good quality contact: vulnerability, mutuality, and openness. We refer to this dimension as the *intimately connected* aspect. The guiding image in this thread is Martin Buber's vision of dialogue (discussed in Chapter 1) which involves intimate, mutually vulnerable, and mutually risk-taking relationships. This is dialogue in which each party is willing to risk their well-staked-out positions and defenses in order to dig deep in seeking a true and meaningful connection. In this way, the persons participating in the dialogue seek to be seen, known, and understood and, through contact and empathy, to see, know, and understand each other. Barriers to contact in the intimately connected aspect frequently involve shame. The aesthetic of the intimately connected aspect reflects the messiness of connection, vulnerability, rupture, and repair.

We have come to value an approach to *relational development* in GGT that appreciates and balances both self-activating and intimately connected qualities and aesthetics. We have experienced time and again the client with an underdeveloped self-activating aspect usually having corresponding difficulties with the intimately connected aspect, and vice versa. Further, we have found that moving beyond the hot seat/open seat in our group work, with a new attention to the group-as-a-whole, has helped clients and trainees develop a greater facility with a relationality that encompasses both the self-activating and intimately connected aspects of development.

Working with the Group-as-a-Whole

Working with the group-as-a-whole involves viewing the group as a complex system that, like a family system, has its own overt and covert rules, norms, and demands. Since each member of the group (including the leader) is part of the group-as-a-whole, having the gestalt group function in as healthy a way as possible is in the interest of everyone. All groups, just as all individuals, have both healthy, functional tendencies, which facilitate the work of the group, and unhealthy, dysfunctional tendencies, which impede it. To work effectively with the group-as-a-whole, we find that it is important to encourage open, ongoing feedback and dialogue within the group about both of these tendencies as they play out in the group process. We expressly support this feedback and dialogue so that a culture may form that respects and values all group members in the co-creation of a healthy, functional group that facilitates relational development.

We ask that group members attend to and voice their feelings about the group-as-a-whole. We encourage members to reflect on and discuss whole group issues such as the safety level in the group, unspoken rules and norms that people aren't talking about (yet feel constrained by), "elephants in the room" (issues which feel too dangerous to give voice to), negative feelings about the leaders, and a whole range of issues that may be forming in the background of the group. In so doing, our goal is not to become a perfect group that has no problems, but rather to work toward being a group that can talk about our problems, challenges, and difficulties.

Another technique that we use in working with the group-as-a-whole is to offer our observations, conjectures, interpretations, and hunches as points of inquiry and dialogue in the group. Statements such as, "I'm aware that Mary is frequently becoming the focus of the group's attention in sharing her despair; I'm wondering if we as a group are coming to rely on her to express these kinds of feelings," may be made to the group. In voicing such a question, the leader is not insisting that this perspective be adopted by the group as "the truth"; instead, the leader is respectfully offering an idea for everyone's consideration. In the spirit of dialogue, the leader is then open to what comes up for group members in response to this. Dialogue around this question might evolve into an object of contemplation: "Do you resonate with the feeling of despair Mary is describing?" An invitation might follow, such as, "Would you be willing to share those feelings with the group?"

Group Process

Group process refers to an ongoing dialogue among all group participants, including the leaders. This ongoing dialogue includes feedback, resonances, confrontations, imaginings, and all manner of thought and feeling that emerge in the experience together. When referring to the group process, we are particularly focused on here-and-now interactions that are occurring in the group (Feder, 2006).

With a focus on what is happening in the here and now of the group process, the relationships here in the room become a primary source of learning, growth, experiment, and change. The complex relational cloth being woven in group members' experiences of each other, of the leaders, and of themselves enriches the group experience and provides many valuable opportunities for growth and integration. In working more creatively with the group process, and enlisting group members in this as well, we have found that our groups have become safer, more honest, more egalitarian, and livelier. Relationality, in its self-activating and intimately connected aspects, seems to have strengthened and deepened, our clients' lives seem to have improved, and our groups feel to us like healthier environments.

In his article, "In Pursuit of Gestalt Therapy Group Process: Group Process as Self Process" (2008), Dan Bloom provides an understanding of group process grounded in gestalt therapy theory. Bloom explores some essential aspects of gestalt therapy theory and shows how they provide excellent ground for an understanding of group process. Bloom's definitions and arguments are very precise and we cannot do his article justice here. Here is our very brief summary:

1. *Self* is the process of contacting the world and synthesizing experience—so the act of being in process is fundamental to our very existence as human beings.
2. Self is embedded in its social surround and is explicitly social and relational.

3. Self is an emergent property of the phenomenal field in which "I" and "we" are both embedded.

4. "Group process" is the attention group members pay to each other in (group) process as (self) process.

What we have taken from Bloom's article is that, from a gestalt therapy perspective, everything is in process, including individuals and groups. We are all fully embedded in our social surround, and the idea of an individual existing outside of his or her social surround is really an absurd abstraction. The individual arises from the social field in which he or she is embedded, and sometimes in the group process the individual aspects of self will come to the fore, whereas at other times it is the collective aspect of self which occupies the foreground. Group process then can be understood to occur when a group of people come together with the intention of attending to each other as human beings who are always in a process of being: both in their embeddedness and their individuality.

For group members to be in connection with each other, and aware of each other as human beings whose very essence is not fixed but always unfolding, is no small undertaking. It is the essence of group process. It requires a high level of safety and containment. It involves empathy, risk-taking, trust, and commitment. In the nine principles of GGT practice we discuss below, we attempt to map the territory of working creatively and effectively with the gestalt therapy group process that Bloom has pointed us to.

Nine Principles of Gestalt Group Therapy Practice

We have organized the rest of this chapter around nine principles that have emerged for us in the practice of a process-oriented GGT:

1. A relational group culture supports each member's relational development.

2. The co-creation of a safe container is a support for the intimately connected aspect of relational development.

3. The leader's attention shifts and flows between three levels of experience in the group: the individual level, the dyadic level, and the group-as-a-whole level.

4. Tension between a relational/contactful position and an alienated/contact-avoidant position shows up at the individual, dyadic, and group-as-a-whole levels in GGT.

5. Holding, listening, and resonating are key functions of the group leader.

6. The leader's awareness of her own gestalt formation process is her most powerful instrument of group leadership.

7. When the leader holds the tension of the polarities, in the spirit of the paradoxical theory of change, she helps the group hold complexity, which in turn becomes fertile ground for the emergence of symbolizing.

8. The *affective current* is the water GGT swims in; *affective processing* is the work of GGT.

9. Dialogue around rupture and repair of the selfobject tie is an ongoing process in GGT.

These principles reflect in particular our focus on relational development in GGT. We will discuss each in turn and illustrate with some case examples as we go.

A Relational Group Culture Supports Each Member's Relational Development

Human growth and development do not occur in isolation. Relational growth and development are the hard-won rewards of staying open to and connected with others. We need relational connection in order to think clearly about our lives, to connect with our feelings, to shuttle between our inner and outer worlds, and to develop our capacities for self-support (i.e., the self-activating aspect) and contactfulness (i.e., the intimately connected aspect). We need relational connection to help us support joy, sexuality, and excitement. We need relational connection in order to bear the suffering that is an inevitable part of our human condition. We need relational connection in order to develop compassion. We need relational connection in order to develop personal power that is balanced with empathy and compassion.

Living relationally, however, entails the sometimes painful and often terrifying process of opening to others. There are, of course, myriad challenges and difficulties involved in opening to others. These include the very real dangers of betrayal, abandonment, destructive competition, seduction, or humiliation at the hands of others who have not done sufficient work on themselves to have become reasonably safe partners on the journey of relatedness. And there are the considerable difficulties involved in changing our own patterns of relating—patterns that have served to protect us in a great many ways from the insults, deceptions, neglect, and abandonments we may have faced in both childhood and adulthood. The contact disturbances so well known to gestalt therapists— confluence, introjection, projection, retroflection, etc.—all serve in one way or another to protect us from these kinds of hurt. They are our creative adjustments to life in an often hurtful world, and these adaptations shape our style of contact-making in the present moment, defining and circumscribing our capacity for relatedness over time.

This brings us to the relational culture that we seek to co-create in GGT. We endeavor to create a safe-enough space for members to form deeply meaningful, intimately connected relationships between themselves, and to explore the feelings and disturbances affecting good quality contact that arise in relation to the hurts, attractions, difficulties, and ruptures that emerge in the group. Within this relational culture, group members are provided with the "safe emergency" of a vital group process in which all the positive and negative feelings that get stirred up in the experience can be intensively explored and worked with. We do not seek a utopian experience in the group culture. Instead, we presuppose that all the difficulties of life will find their way into the group, and that the group, with its support for speaking truth, can and will provide encouragement for members in opening up to a wider range of possibilities of how they experience, how they relate, and how they choose. Our goal is to foster an atmosphere of awareness, reflection, and connection that is safe enough to work on life's riskiest material.

The Co-creation of a Safe Container is a Support for the Intimately Connected Aspect of Relational Development

As group members become increasingly connected through their participation in the group process, passions, vulnerabilities, and previously covered-over sensitivities tend to come to the fore. This is exactly what we want to occur, as group members can more readily do the work of integration and change when they are in touch with their vulnerabilities and fixed gestalts in the here and now of the group process. However, bringing forth this kind of material in the group often puts group members in a state of vulnerability, and group boundaries are an important support to this kind of opening. We think of group boundaries that support enough safety to do life's riskiest work as the co-creation of a safe and strong container.

> Jim is a 45-year-old married college professor who revealed in the group his attraction to another group member, Mary, a 32-year-old single nurse. Jim experienced this disclosure as extremely risky, as he had strongly suppressed the sexual feelings that contact with some of his female students had stirred in him. His sexual desires were deeply hidden from others, and were causing him great strife, conflict, and guilt. Bringing his feelings of attraction to another group member into the group process was a courageous act that carried with it both a positive potential for growth and healing in his sexuality and a negative potential for experiencing shame and pushing his sexual issues deeper into hiding.

For her part, the feelings that Jim revealed about her hit a nerve for Mary. She had recently shared in group about casual sexual involvements with men she had been meeting at bars. She was quite ambivalent about these liaisons. Jim's confession brought forth a conflicted mix of feelings for her. She felt pleasure and excitement at being desired by Jim, yet she felt shame about her earlier sharing concerning her casual sexual encounters, and discomfort that perhaps Jim had been titillated by her earlier sharing and that he was now only seeing her as a sexual object.

In this example we can begin to see the potential for growth, along with the difficulties, sensitivities, and complexities that arise when we engage with the intimately connected aspect of relational development in the group. The intimately connected aspect often carries with it a vital current of sexuality, and in GGT these feelings need to find safe expression. The question for us to consider here is how to make this kind of sharing safe enough so that both Jim and Mary, as well as the rest of the group, can productively explore and discuss issues that have the potential to bring up both the excitement and the shame that intimate and sexual issues frequently evoke.

This brings us to a discussion of the safe container. For both Jim and Mary, engaging in this dialogue requires well-defined boundaries, or what we refer to as a *safe and strong container*. In order to proceed with her explorations, Mary needs to trust that Jim is not going to approach her outside the group for a relationship, and both Jim and Mary must trust that group members are going to maintain confidentiality. The GGT leader must address the boundaries and rules that promote a sense that the group is safe enough to support the risky work of opening up in the intimately connected dimension.

As a practical matter, we do not have a rigid set of rules that we follow with every group, as different groups call for different boundaries. For example, training groups require different boundaries than treatment groups, and groups for people with personality disorders may require different rules from groups for high-functioning people. However, here are some basic guidelines that we follow:

- Maintaining confidentiality is a basic and fundamental commitment that each group member is required to make.
- If group members have contact outside the group, they commit to not gossiping about other group members in that contact, and they commit to talking with the group about that contact.
- Group is not a place to search out or pursue sexual partnerships.
- Communication is expressed non-abusively.

Of course, there is a great deal more to the co-creation of a safe container than the level of bottom-line behaviors that are to be avoided. In fact, all of the principles in this chapter can be thought of as supports to the co-creation of a safe and strong container. Nevertheless, we have found that the clear articulation of the rules of the group is a support. Frequently, there will be much discussion and dialogue around the group boundaries. When rules are broken, this is important grist for the mill. We welcome these discussions as they promote the co-creation of a safe and strong container.

> As it turned out, Jim and Mary spent a good deal of time on these issues, and both grew from the experience. Both were able to talk about the feelings evoked, and both observed the boundaries of the group, so that they were able to risk and grow in the dialogue. Over time, Jim grew more accepting of his sexual attraction to Mary and confident that he could hold and integrate these feelings without either suppressing them or acting on them; he learned to "hold a charge." On campus, in his work, he developed a greater capacity to accept his desires as part and parcel of his human condition rather than as a source of shame. Mary, in turn, learned much about her responses to men, and discovered a greater capacity for holding her own when faced with a man and his desire for her.

The Leader's Attention Shifts and Flows between Three Levels of Experience in the Group: The Individual, Dyadic, and Group-as-a-Whole

We generally work with individual-level issues in the familiar mode of one-on-one work between the leader and a group member. Dyadic issues involve two group members who have an issue between them that needs the support of the group to get sorted out. Group-as-a-whole issues involve everyone in the group as a family or system in which we deal with problems such as splitting, individuals getting pushed into certain stereotyped roles, group norms, and so on.

Individual Level

A piece of individual work with the leader in our current group work looks a lot like it would have in our "hot seat/open seat" days. We have not thrown out the baby with the bathwater, and there is still room in our groups for a hot-seat piece of work with the leader. However, there is more flow now, in that pieces of individual work seem to flow into the dyadic and group-as-a-whole levels that involve other members much more readily.

Broadly speaking, we would include the working through of a feeling between a group member and the leader in the category of individual work. Frequently when one group member is working with a feeling toward the leader, other group members will also be stimulated to work with such feelings by way of empathy and/or resonance, and an individual-level piece of work might easily flow into group-as-a-whole work.

Dyadic Level

Work at the dyadic level can be very exciting and broadening for the group members involved and for the entire group. Work between two people can be useful and productive when:

1.   Difficulties arise between two group members, such as when one member experiences another member's comment as a put-down.
2.   A connection develops between two group members that they wish to explore, such as a sexual attraction.
3.   There is a shared feeling or experience between two group members, such as two women, both of whom had abandoning fathers, who together explore their experiences, feelings, and styles of making contact with men.

Group-as-a-Whole Level

Work at the group-as-a-whole level is looking at the whole group as a system. At this level, both group members and group leaders track how the group feels and how we are functioning. We look at developments, such as ways in which group members are enlisted by the group into playing out certain roles and thereby carry feelings in the group that other members are not owning. In group therapy theory, it is said that individuals may have a *valency* for carrying a feeling for the group (Bion, 1960; Rutan, Stone, & Shay, 2007). For example, one member might have a valency for carrying the group's anger at the leader. Another might have a valency for carrying the group's sexuality or the group's depression. A person could have a valency for being excluded or blamed. It should be noted that a valency is not simply the individual projecting his usual issues onto the group. Instead, a valency is the individual's vulnerability to enacting something powerful, in which the group and the individual collude, with varying degrees of awareness, to manifest something that is being otherwise disowned by group members.

Tiffany had a valency for being treated with quiet disdain by other members of a therapy group. Her drug-addicted mother had died of an overdose when Tiffany was just 12, and she was raised by her father

and stepmother, who subsequently had three more children. Her stepmother never treated Tiffany well, and excluded her from the love and
protection she provided her biological children. Tiffany's half-siblings
were often cruel to her. Tiffany had adopted a whining, self-pitying,
oral, needy style in her group relationships that left others feeling
annoyed and impatient with her. The group had found in Tiffany a
person who would enact the scapegoat role—someone onto whom
their unwanted, disavowed qualities could be projected and disowned.
Tiffany's valency for feeling and becoming left out and needy blended
with the group's primitive need for a scapegoat who held their contempt and disdain, and a full-fledged enactment was underway.

The beauty of a group-as-a-whole perspective and intervention
in this type of enactment is that it involves everyone in the group.
Tiffany's oral/needy style of making contact is only a part of the
problem, and working with this without looking at the group's part
can further scapegoat her. Involving the whole group in reflection
on this material helps further everyone in the group's growth, and
allows Tiffany an experience of being part of a group that will look
at and try to own its shadow side. Further healing may occur as
group members try to take responsibility for their own behavior. This
owning of their part may open the door for Tiffany to look at her
off-putting style of relating to others in the group.

We asked the whole group to look at what Tiffany might be holding for the group in expressing feelings of being left out in the cold
and wanting. As group members shared their experiences of feeling
left in need, both in the group and in their lives, the pressure lifted
off Tiffany, and she was able to explore new ways of making contact
with other group members.

Another benefit of the group-as-a-whole perspective is that it can be helpful in the reduction of shame. Shame reduction can occur when the group
leaders seek to involve the whole group in issues that have caused shame
for a particular group member.

Ethan revealed to the group his addiction to high-risk sexual behavior
with sex workers. On revealing this to the group, he began to experience a strong shame response. A simple group-as-a-whole intervention was to thank him for being so courageous in bringing this into
the group, and to praise his leadership in the group by taking risks
in going deeper with his sharing. This opened the door for others to
share sexual secrets that they had been keeping. In highlighting the
leadership that Ethan was providing for the group-as-a-whole, his
sharing of material that might have brought him increased shame
instead brought him relief and a sense of greater closeness with other

group members, who were able to follow his lead and share sensitive sexual material with the group.

Tension between a Relational/Contactful Position and an Alienated/Contact-Avoidant Position Shows Up at the Individual, Dyadic, and Group-as-a-Whole Levels in GGT

A basic polarity we work with in GGT is living our lives in the rich, dynamic uncertainty of a relational/contactful position as opposed to seeking the safety and apparent self-sufficiency of assuming an alienated/contact-avoidant position. From the relational/contactful position, we seek to know others and to be known, to grow in compassion, to be open and creative. From the alienated/contact-avoidant position, we defend ourselves from others, we strive for control, and we stake out our positions rather than tolerating the uncertainty of searching for our truth. From the relational/contactful position, we accept the pain that comes with connection, honesty, and humility. From the alienated/contact-avoidant position, we protect ourselves from pain through avoidance of intimacy and connection.

Let us look at how this basic polarity manifests at the individual, dyadic, and group-as-a-whole levels.

Individual Level: The Ongoing Choice to Live from a Relational/Contactful Position versus the Choice to Live from an Alienated/Contact-avoidant Position

Individual participants in GGT face a particular tension that each group member works with in her own way, within her own context, and with her own ongoing choices. The "safe" choice is to remain hidden, to protect ourselves through a variety of strategies that lead to disconnection, alienation, and contact avoidance. Getting stuck in the alienated/contact-avoidant position keeps us safe, but exacts a terrible penalty—our slow but inexorable drift away from integration and connection. It is through choosing relationality and contactful living that we develop and integrate our many selves, our many feeling states (Polster, 1995). Getting stuck in the contact-avoidant position blocks us from the self-development that occurs in the vulnerability of relationality and connection. We all have strivings toward contactful relatedness and countervailing tendencies toward contact-avoidant alienation. In balance and integration, contact avoidance is transformed from a static and stuck state of disconnection from others into healthy, temporary withdrawal from contact that supports ongoing relationship, similar to Zinker's (1998) phase of withdrawal within the cycle of experience.

We do not seek resolution of this fundamental tension, for each person will always have both tendencies to choose relatedness and other tendencies to choose alienation. The gestalt group, with its feedback, long-term relationships, care, and honesty, is an ideal setting for learning more about these choices, which we all share and must work with. Again, our therapeutic goal is not the resolution of life's problems so much as the development of a self that can continue to learn, grow, and love in the face of life's contradictions, disappointments, losses, and polarities. We do not seek victory of the relational/contactful position over the alienated/contact-avoidant position. Instead, we work to highlight this polarity as an ongoing choice of working toward connection, while also appreciating the tendency to isolate. We help our clients identify the difference between withdrawal in the service of relationship, and isolation that works against relationship.

The gestalt group therapist works to hold, appreciate, and open up dialogue around the polarity of choosing the relational/contactful position versus the alienated/contact-avoidant position. Frequently, this material will show up in group members' plans to leave the group, in low commitment to doing the work of the group, in coming late, in staying silent about major life issues, and other manifestations of ambivalence.

> Sally was in individual and group therapy with me [Daisy]. She had been missing group rather frequently since her mother had taken ill. She talked about her mother's illness in individual therapy but did not tell the group about it. As we explored this in her individual sessions, Sally said that her mother's illness was "too personal to share in the group." As we began to explore what "too personal to share" meant to Sally, she said that she would feel extremely vulnerable in group if people knew how distressed she was about her mother's illness. Sally became aware of an introject from her Irish-American family that talking to outsiders about family issues was a sign of weakness, and that strong people remain silent. This awareness led to a good deal of work around how she keeps people at arm's length and thereby misses out on much richness and support. Working with these issues in her individual therapy created an opening for Sally to talk with the group about her mother's illness and her own distress around it. She worked with accepting support from other group members and with taking in the group's love and support as a source of resilience and strength rather than as a sign of weakness.

Dyadic Level: The Tension between the Relational/Contactful Position and the Alienated/Contact-avoidant Position often Shows Up in the Interactions between Two Group Members

Issues that arise between two group members will frequently have a feeling of intensity for one or both members, evoking conflict, competition, or attraction. Supporting both members of the dyad in staying related to each other even in the face of strong feelings can enhance relationship and contact.

As a child, Patrick had been molested by a teacher. Additionally, his mother had been very sexually stimulating toward him throughout his childhood. As an adult, Patrick had a great deal of difficulty in forming and maintaining intimate relationships with women. When he described himself in typically self-deprecating terms, Chloe, an attractive group member, told Patrick that she liked him and was disturbed by how he put himself down. Patrick raised a hand, palm out—like a traffic cop signaling "stop"—and went on to a quite defensive exposition about how she had "not heard him." I [Peter] intervened in this exchange with the hope of slowing down the interaction so that we could work with it. I reflected back to Patrick the gesture he had made that looked like a cop stopping traffic, and asked him to try the gesture again with awareness, and to put words to what his hand was saying to Chloe. This time he raised his hand and said to Chloe, "This is getting scary and I need you to stop." I asked him to stay with it, and to see if he might say what was scary. "I'm not used to talking with women this way. I like Chloe and I get shy when a woman likes me back." I asked if it would be all right to hear from Chloe. Chloe shared her surprise and delight that Patrick liked her. She had had no idea, and said that she thought he found her annoying. The fact that Patrick liked her was particularly important to Chloe, as she had quite a lot of difficulty in her relationships with men, and was confused about how men responded to her.Patrick and Chloe were both energized, blushing, and smiling. I asked Patrick to attend to his body—to what he felt. He shared a sense of pleasure and excitement in his physical body and an emotional sense of expansiveness. Chloe shared her sense of feeling hot, flushed, and engaged. I asked Patrick to attend to the moment, to the experience of feeling pleasure and staying engaged. I asked him to let her in visually, and to talk with her about what he was feeling. He talked with Chloe about his experience and then told me that this was enough. Chloe had had enough too, and the intense contact between them came to a pleasing end. Over the ensuing weeks, both Patrick and Chloe shared progress they had made in dating and relationships. Although they didn't connect their progress with the work they were doing in group, we felt that perhaps their increased capacity for pleasure in the group was helping them both with their intimate lives.

In supporting group members at the dyadic level of contact-making, the GGT leader helps to make the group more immediate and more contactful by helping to support moments of meeting between two group members. The polarity of the relational/contactful position versus the alienated/contact-avoidant position often plays out at the dyadic level with an intensity and passion that enlivens the whole group.

Group-as-a-Whole Level: The Tension between the Relational/Contactful Position and the Alienated/Contact-avoidant Position often Shows Up with Healthy, Fluid Subgrouping versus Factionalizing, Splitting, and Unhealthy Subgrouping

There is an unfortunate tendency in human groups to split and factionalize. In groups, people have a primitive tendency to split into opposing camps. Splitting shows up as a boundary disturbance in GGT, as it calls forth confluence between members on one side of the split and projection onto those on the other side of the split. We have learned through hard experience that what can look to the leader like a happy and copacetic group can feel to group members like a junior high school dance, rife with unspoken alliances, hurts, and destructive competition. Much of this suffering is due to hidden splitting and factionalizing. We have learned to look for signs of this kind of splitting—it may show up subtly in the form of interruptions, group members who rarely respond to other group members, or reactivity between subgroups.

On the healthy side of the coin, *fluid* subgrouping can be quite beneficial. With fluid subgrouping we seek to avail ourselves of the benefits inherent to subgrouping—the support that members can receive through alliances and special connections and the support of finding others with similar difficulties and pains. But while supporting healthy subgrouping, we stay alert to splitting and factionalizing that can turn a group into an emotionally dangerous environment. Furthermore, we pay attention to the tendency of such subgroups to become stuck and intractably opposing camps. Fluid subgrouping means that people can be in one subgroup, made up of a certain group of members in one discussion, but can flow into another subgroup with another group of members with the next discussion. This flow in subgrouping makes splitting and projecting less problematic, because the person who was outside of one's subgroup a minute ago may now be a member of one's new subgroup. Primitive projections have less opportunity to take hold when the membership in various subgroupings is dynamically changing.

When we observe that the group is splitting into opposing camps, that members are being subjected to scapegoating or other kinds of unhealthy projection, or when there is a generalized low energy or malaise or persistent conflict in the group, we will often adopt a group-as-a-whole intervention aimed at an exploration of splitting and unhealthy subgrouping in an effort to restore a greater sense of relatedness.

In a therapy group for therapists, three group members were talking after the group outside the building on the street. A fourth group member, Ruth, walked out of the building, saw them, and tried to join their discussion. She felt that they were unwelcoming of her. Ruth went home feeling hurt and rejected. She was quite angry at the next group, accusing the other group members of being hurtful. The other three group members in turn were surprised and offended by Ruth's accusation. Two other group members took Ruth's side, and a full-scale split in the group was well on its way to forming. The next few sessions brought further bad feeling between the two camps. We discussed this issue with our consultation group, and came to an understanding that splitting into these two warring camps was pulling the group away from a relational/contactful position and toward an alienated/contact-avoidant position. We offered this perspective to the group: that we as a group were avoiding the work of staying connected and opening up through splitting and fighting. We asked the group to explore feelings and issues that were going unattended because of the group's conflict. This exploration opened the door to new personal sharing from group members, new connections being made, and new fluid connections and subgroups forming on the basis of support rather than getting stuck in opposing camps that had been engaged in projection and conflict. As we worked our way through this impasse, all parties were eventually able to come back to the events that caused the initial bad feeling and repair the rupture that had occurred.

Holding, Listening, and Resonating are Key Functions of the Group Leader

In doing the work of holding, listening, and resonating, the leader is like a musical instrument. Just as the body of a guitar holds the strings at a certain tension and brings the beauty of their sound forward into the room, so does the leader hold the group, listen to the feelings the group members share, resonate with those feelings, and bring the reverberations back to the group for all to feel and consider. With the leader's attention to holding and resonance, group members can actively learn, grow, explore, and develop together. The full spectrum of life—life that is happening in and around the group and its individual members—animates the group so that the work of the group may unfold.

Foreground functions of the GGT leader include intervening, proposing experiments, and doing individual pieces of work. The background functions of holding, listening, and resonating are equally important. The Lacanian psychoanalyst and Marxist philosopher, Slavoj Žižek (2011), has made the point that what the world needs now is less action and more thinking. He suggests that we need to put less focus on action and more focus on formulating the right questions. In the arena of GGT we find his advice on point.

Here, then, are some reflections on these important background functions of GGT leadership.

Holding

Have you ever noticed the difference between a facilitated group and a peer group? In our experience, these two kinds of group can feel very different from each other. In the facilitated group, there is someone who is endowed by the group with the responsibility to participate in the group experience in a very particular way. The leader *holds* the group. The leader participates differently from the other members. The leader holds the space, listens for how the group is functioning, tunes into the feeling tone of the group, reflects on the group process, and assumes greater responsibility for the welfare of the group. In the leaderless group, there tends to be less safety, less reflection on the process, and more difficulty in productively confronting the people and issues in the group that must be dealt with in order for the group to function well.

Listening

Most of our time spent in group leadership is spent listening. We listen to the group members. We listen to our fantasies. We listen to the group as a whole. We listen actively. We watch our ability to track what is happening in the group wax and wane. We listen to the music playing in our minds and wonder what it is saying about the group. And we wait for integrative awareness to form inside —an awareness that lends energy to an intervention, musing, interpretation, or experiment.

One reason that we are turned off to formulaic approaches to group therapy, and one of the reasons we love the gestalt approach, is that we cherish GGT's emphasis on creativity, spontaneity, and freedom. Therefore, we are very interested in how the therapist listens. How we take in the people and information is fundamental to how we integrate and work creatively with the material that comes up in the group. And this is deeply personal. We encourage all GGT leaders to think deeply about how you listen to others and how you attend to your own inner muse.

One rule of thumb is that whatever is inside of you—in your body and mind, when you are sitting with the group in the leader's chair—is information about the group. We encourage you to listen to what gets activated inside of you and ask yourself, "What is this telling me about this group?" By the way, the things that get stirred up in me are often quite silly or banal, yet these little fantasies tell me so much.

> I [Peter] was sitting with a group that was in a stuck place, but no one was talking about the real problems in the group. I found myself fantasizing that everybody was just going to quit the group. Then I went into a memory of a story from a cop show called *Homicide*, which I'd seen years ago, in which an elderly man kills his wife. After much investigating, the cops figure out that the man had started up an affair with his high-school sweetheart and had killed his wife to get out of the marriage so that he could take up with this other woman. The cops ask him, "Why didn't you just ask her for a divorce instead of killing her in cold blood?" The man replies, "I didn't want to hurt her feelings!"
>
> I tell this story to the group, and suggest that it is telling me that perhaps we in the group would rather kill the group than speak the difficult, unsettling truth. Following my disclosure, the energy in the group picked up dramatically, and a series of difficult interpersonal issues involving everyone in the group came out and got worked with, and the group ended the session in a much livelier, more contactful place.

Resonating

Let us return to the metaphor of the group leader as the body of a guitar, group members as the strings of the guitar, and life itself as the musician. In this metaphor, the leader's most important job is to hold and resonate. Just as the guitar holds the strings at a certain tension to enable them to sound, the leader holds the group members with her presence, her attention, her boundaries, and her dedication to the group. This holding then allows members to share their thoughts, feelings, and somatic states, and to bring their inner lives into the group space.

The leader resonates with the material that group members bring. She reflects back to the group the feelings that are present in the group, and, through her resonance, group members have the opportunity to see themselves in a new light. For example, in our co-ed group, several members talk about scary things: an engineer feels he might be replaced by a computerized tool; a physician feels that she might be getting too old to practice and not make mistakes; a mother frets about her depressed daughter. Our resonance to these feelings is that the group is that special place where we can bring our private worries and concerns and have them held without judgment or advice. When the group hears this resonance, they express appreciation and love for each other, and a new feeling of strength and confidence seems to emerge.

The Leader's Awareness of Her Own Gestalt Formation Process is Her Most Powerful Instrument of Group Leadership

Zinker (1977) has written about the gestalt formation process. Philippson (2009) has written about emergent properties. In this section, we will look at the GGT leader's gestalt formation as an emergent property of the gestalt group. In the gestalt formation process, we become aware of what is inside of us, and we try on the idea that what is inside is connected with, and in some ways a function of, the field or the group. When we GGT leaders develop our own processes of thinking about our gestalt formation process as a function of the group process, then we are truly doing the work of deepening the dialogue in the group.

According to Zinker (1977), and modified slightly by us in Chapter 1 of this book, the gestalt formation process goes through the following phases: sensation, awareness, mobilization of energy, action, contact/change, and new equilibrium. Below is an example of how the leader's gestalt formation process serves as an important function of group leadership, where the gestalts that form for the leader can be understood as emerging from the group process.

Sensation—Leah abruptly announces that she is planning to leave a therapist group she has been a long-term member of. In the moment of her announcement, Daisy and I both have vaguely sad, anxious, and disappointed feelings about her leaving.

Awareness—After the group, Daisy and I share with each other these feelings of disappointment about Leah's decision to leave the group, and together we find that we feel caught in a dilemma. On the one hand, we don't want to be coercive by trying to influence her to stay. On the other hand, we feel that she may be choosing to leave because of issues that have been brewing under the surface of the group. Specifically, we feel that Leah might be wanting greater intensity and intimacy in the group, which we feel the group has been avoiding.

Mobilization of energy—We take the issue to our consultation group, and hear from others about the issue. We decide that we are going to talk with Leah about it at the next session.

Action—We tell Leah of our dilemma—that on the one hand we respect her decision and do not want to be heavy-handed or coercive about her leaving, but on the other hand we have some reservations. We ask if she is all right with us expressing our reservations, which she is.

Contact/change—Daisy shares thoughts and fantasies about what may be going on for Leah in relation to the group, and also explores feelings that Leah may be having toward Daisy and me. This becomes quite an intense piece of individual work with good quality contact, and much is explored about the group and how we function, so that the individual work is of great interest to all group participants. Leah expresses much about the group, herself, her relationships, her marriage, and her feelings toward Daisy and me. Group members get deeply engaged in the dialogue, and after a time enter in with their thoughts, feelings, and resonances to the work. Leah decides to stay with the group.

New equilibrium—After this piece of work, there is a renewal of cohesiveness in the group (Yalom, 1995) and a sense of connectedness that draws the members together. For our part, Daisy and I feel satisfied that we worked with the sad/anxious/disappointed feelings we had when Leah announced that she was leaving. Soon another piece of work begins, and other gestalts start forming for Daisy and me, as well as for the group members. But the new work is informed by the work Leah has just done, and a process of developing complexity and mastery is palpable in the room, bringing greater support for the emergence of new, complex issues within the group. The group has integrated Leah's work and is now ready to move into more intimacy and intensity with each other.

When the Leader Holds the Tension of the Polarities, in the Spirit of the Paradoxical Theory of Change, She Helps the Group Hold Complexity, Which in Turn becomes Fertile Ground for the Emergence of Symbolizing

Beisser (1971, p. 77) articulated gestalt therapy's paradoxical theory of change thus:

> [C]hange occurs when one becomes what he is, not when he tries to become what he is not. Change does not take place through a coercive attempt by the individual or by another person to change him, but it does take place if one takes the time and effort to be what he is—to be fully invested in his current positions.

Note here that Beisser uses the plural "positions," indicating that the current situation may well be one of polarities and conflict rather than a unitary position.

The paradoxical theory of change provides an excellent framework for working with the many polarities that show up in GGT. Although we usually think of the paradoxical theory of change in terms of the individual who is willfully trying to impose change on himself, it also applies in GGT as a reminder to the leader that our job is not so much to find resolution to the polarities and complexities that our members present but rather to hold the complexity, to support the group member in taking the time to be exactly who he is, to be fully invested in his current positions, even when those positions are contradictory and are seemingly at polar opposites. The paradoxical theory of change reminds us that change is more an act of integration than of will, and that, when we hold the complexity of the contradictions, new awareness may well emerge.

Earlier we discussed the basic polarity of the relational/contactful position versus the alienated/contact-avoidant position. Let us now look at polarities themselves as a phenomenon of the psyche. Perls pointed out that psychological states of being and identifications come in sets of opposites. Thus, for example, Perls (1973) pointed out that the harsh, perfectionist topdog has its opposite in the flawed yet human underdog. We see an unending series of polarities in people such as: the sanctimoniously religious man who leads a secret sexual life; the kind, sensitive "earth mother" who secretly carries grudges and resentments; the modest wife who secretly encourages her husband's abuses of power; the socially responsible, politically progressive inheritor who secretly disdains those without wealth and power. And, of course, sometimes the less socially acceptable aspects are visible, and the "virtuous" side is hidden, such as the ruthless businessman who secretly has a loving, compassionate, soft side, or the pushy, overly ambitious mother who suppresses her kindness.

In GGT we do not seek resolution of life's contradictions, problems, and complexity. We do not seek cure. Rather, we seek a deeper relationship with the issues that trouble us and hold us in a state of conflict. We seek the development of a sense of self, a sense that is formed in relationship, a self that can continue to flow and grow even while life's most painful issues, conflicts, and challenges feel overwhelming. Rather than seeking resolution to the conflicts, we seek the development of a self, held in the safety of the group, which can work with the issues and conflicts that arise. If this leads to resolution of a particular difficulty or conflict, we welcome this, but we do not aim for it.

In GGT we work with life's polarities. Additionally, we work with the ways in which unwanted, unintegrated aspects can get projected onto group members. For example, group members may have difficulty integrating their anger, and a member with a valency for carrying the group's anger gets stuck with it, and, in so doing, other group members can reject both their unintegrated anger and the person who is carrying it. This is a form of scapegoating that can easily occur with unintegrated feelings in the group.

The paradoxical theory of change is a great help here. When the leader encourages each member to own his or her own feelings, to fully experience what *is*, then shortcuts such as projecting the feelings onto another group member can be contained, and group members have an opportunity to live in and experience the complexity that accompanies owning both sides of their polarities. This can be difficult for group members who are identified with and invested in seeing only one side of themselves, and are equally invested in suppressing the disowned side of the polarity. Owning both sides of ourselves can be ego-dystonic, humbling, and anxiety-provoking. But in the discomfort of owning our many selves, even the selves that we disapprove of, we open the door to the emergence of something new—a new understanding, a new level of acceptance, a new feeling.

This "something new" is at once the integration of the opposites, the ability to hold opposites as one integrated whole, and something entirely new that emerges from holding the complexity of the opposites. This "something new" is the formation of new gestalts that emerge in the crucible of holding the opposites.[3] This "something new" involves the ability to move from concrete thinking about the polarity to the ability to symbolize. We will discuss the importance of moving from concrete thinking and offer a few case examples below.

Earlier in this chapter we discussed the gestalt formation process along the lines of Zinker's (1977) cycle of experience. We propose here another process that gives rise to a particular kind of gestalt—a gestalt that has emergent properties. In this process of gestalt formation, the opposites are joined and held. This seemingly impossible task—holding both sides of a polarity—is transformative, and gives birth to the new gestalt—a new sense of wholeness based on a fuller sense of self, and a greater awareness of the field. Just as the "primordial soup" of just the right mix of organic compounds, heat, and water gave rise to something new—the first life forms—so does the emergence of a new gestalt formation rise from the holding of the complexity of the opposites. And, as we have said, the new gestalt that forms out of holding the opposites involves the capacity to symbolize the opposites, rather than holding them concretely.

Symbolizing at the Individual Level

Michelle stated many times that she cared for and valued the group and all the people in it, yet she did numerous things that were harmful to the group, such as missing sessions, not paying the fee on time, coming late, creating splits and divisions in the group, and being unwelcoming to new members. When we spoke to her about these behaviors, and shared our curiosity about the feelings underneath, she deflected us. Over time, however, with continued dialogue with the leaders and other group members, she began to own and identify with these destructive tendencies, tying them in with the sexual abuse she suffered in childhood and the creative adjustments she had made to survive a dangerous childhood filled with trauma. In owning the destructive side, and holding at the same time the part of her that did indeed love and need the group, Michelle was holding the tension of the opposites, and she and the whole group were holding the complexity of her experience. What emerged from this was a new gestalt, a different sense of self that was at once more flexible, less brittle, more human, and less perfectionistic than the old sense of self. With this new sense of self, she no longer needed to deflect dialogue about her destructive side, but was able to hear it, take responsibility, and symbolize the behavior.

One of the characteristics of new gestalts that emerge from holding the complexity of the opposites is the ability to symbolize. To symbolize is to be able to hold the whole, to connect the present impulse and behavior with history, to hold what triggers us with a sense of what it means to us.

When Michelle was able to hold the opposites—caring for and needing the group on the one hand, yet being destructive to the group on the other hand—holding both of these polarities came with the ability to symbolize the complex feelings that her growing attachment to the group was activating in her. She connected her attachment to the group to her attachments in her family of origin, where her narcissistic mother and abusive father failed miserably in their ability to empathize with her in childhood. She played the obedient child who perfectly mirrored her narcissistic parents on the outside, but inside she was afraid, hurt, and seething with anger. Her destructive behavior had been an enactment of the rage she felt as a child in having to swallow abuse and neglect in order to get whatever good things were available in her family. When she was able to symbolize and make these connections, she could share with the group the intense feelings that came up for her as she felt her growing attachment to the group, its members, and leaders. The group in turn was able to listen, hold her, and help her connect with these feelings while staying connected with the rest of the group. This growing capacity to hold the opposites and symbolize translated into better relationships for Michelle at her work and in her family life.

Symbolizing as a Group

Matt brings a problem to the group: he cannot mobilize himself to clean his house or throw things away. He has been hoarding, and can barely move around in his house. His topdog and underdog sides are split. The topdog mercilessly berates him, while the underdog is immobilized, unable to function on this issue. Although he has made a little progress with this issue, he is overwhelmed with feelings of shame. As long as Matt and the group are caught in the topdog/underdog split, the group offers a fruitless and shame-inducing series of "helpful suggestions." The concrete aspect of the issue of his hoarding behavior feels compelling to both Matt and other group members. I [Daisy] sense that we, the group, are missing out on a rich undercurrent of feelings that have been stirred up with this issue. An experiment emerges in my consciousness out of connecting with this complexity. I say to the whole group, "I'd like you all to imagine that Matt's house, filled with clutter, was a dream image in your own dream. How would it feel, and what would it mean to you if this were your dream?"

Now group members feel the call of something deeper and more connecting: what this brings up deep inside of them. Now Matt's issues with his house can be felt in its symbolic dimension. David remembers growing up in a public housing apartment in an otherwise middle-class Los Angeles neighborhood. He remembers being rejected as a child by friends because his family was on welfare. This brings up fear of being rejected by the group as a result of his current financial and work status. It also brings up a feeling of family chaos that has been internalized as a feeling of inferiority with other people. Other group members share feelings and memories that have come up in imagining Matt's house as a dream image. Matt now reports a reduction in shame, and over the next few sessions reports progress with getting his house cleared out, getting his bills paid, and getting his paperwork done at work.

The *Affective Current* is the Water GGT Swims In; Affective Processing is the Work of GGT

We offer the term *affective current* to refer to the ongoing stream of feelings running through each of us at all times. Here we are aware of two meanings of the word *current*—both as a flow of energy and as an occurrence in the present moment. As long as we are alive, the affective current is our emotional energy that is flowing in the now. This affective current includes our mood, our emotional response to the immediate field, the stream of our sexual, libidinal energies, our sense of excitement, danger, attractions, and repulsions that are unfolding within us as we move in and through the flow of life in the present moment.[4]

The *affective current* is the ongoing emotional dimension of the human experience. Common symbols of this ongoing affective current are bodies of water. Oceans, rivers, and lakes often show up in our dreams as symbols of this dimension of our lives: the dimension of feeling, affect, and emotion. This is the water that GGT swims in, and may be thought of as the water of human life itself. We return to this water frequently in group life, getting in touch with the flow of feelings or affective current that is running through the group and its members.

The affective current is the water we swim in but, just as the question of whether the tree that falls in the forest makes a sound when no one is there to hear it, so too must we inquire about the impact of the affective current that occurs outside of awareness. While the affective current is a constant, making *contact* with the affective current is not so common and can be very difficult to achieve. This work can be thought of as the work of life itself. We will refer to the work of making contact with the affective current as *affective processing*. The distinction between *the affective current* and *affective processing* is crucial. Every person has an ongoing flow of feelings inside him or her. This affective current, our organismic response to the field, is natural and ubiquitous. It is a kind of fluid emotional representation of the world that each of us carries within us at all times. The affective current is always powerfully at work, and always colors our subjectivity. When this happens outside of awareness, then we are unaware of the most powerful driver of our perceptions, thinking, and contact-making. This lack of awareness gives rise to much suffering, for it is then that we react to the affective current with boundary disturbances that distort our perceptions, impair our relationships, and impede our capacity to think clearly.

It is the work of GGT to use the power of the group to bring the affective current into awareness. We will call this pursuit of awareness of the affective current *affective processing*. Affective processing is no small undertaking; it is the most important work of GGT. Affective processing is not gained without hard work, self-reflection, and a willingness to endure some suffering. In our clinical practice, we have found that GGT is a potent milieu in which to engage in the work of affective processing. Awareness does not occur in a relational vacuum. Each person needs much support in order to be with and deeply take in the affective life that flows within herself, for the water that we swim in is not placid—it is powerfully passionate. Strong feelings, such as love, hate, desire, need, and abandonment, are not easily integrated. In GGT we provide support for the affective processing that is necessary to bring the affective current into awareness. We do this by working with the individual, dyadic, and group-as-a-whole levels, marshaling support at each of those levels for the challenging work of affective processing. In the self-activating aspect, affective processing helps refine awareness of what we desire to pursue. In the intimately connected aspect, affective processing helps us navigate the complex feelings that help us attach and stay connected with others.

Herein lies the beauty of GGT. In GGT, our purpose is simply to grow more fully into ourselves—we pursue affective processing as a path to the examined, empowered, and relationally rich life. The leaders do not pursue goals such as self-improvement, overcoming depression, losing weight, becoming more successful, or finding the ideal mate in GGT. While many of these things may be welcome, we do not aim for them. What we try to connect with in GGT is the affective processing that brings us into contact with our emotional responses to life. This affective processing, we feel, is the royal road to emotional health.

In relative health, we are better able to connect with and process the affective current so that it informs our large and small choices. In relative ill health, we are dominated by the affective current, but not with awareness. In ill health, with ineffective affective processing, our perceptions of reality, and our capacity for contactful, richly relational living, are limited. When the affective current is insufficiently and ineffectively held, we become alienated from our emotional resonances and bodily responses, so that our inner life becomes a stranger to us. What, with strong affective processing, would be our greatest source of wisdom, instead becomes a fearful, unknown presence that lies at the very core of our subjectivity. When the affective current is unknown, yet so familiar and powerful, it becomes terrifying. Is it any wonder that primitive, fundamentalist religious systems project the fantasy image of Satan onto this dimension of our lives while primitive political systems project the hated and feared "other" onto this aspect of ourselves? Satan or the hated and feared other are perfect symbols of how the affective current can feel to those who do not have the tools of affective processing that transform the raw material of emotion and sensation into wisdom. Outside of awareness, what is inside of us becomes frightening, and, as unfinished business, clamors for our attention and for closure. The affective current becomes ominous and a source of primitive fear, giving rise to projection, splitting, and all manner of suffering. *Affective processing* involves an increasing capacity to stay with our affective current, to hold it with awareness, and to marshal the signals we receive from our ongoing affective current in the service of making richer choices, finding better contact, and staying emotionally connected with others.

In GGT, the leader starts with this basic understanding: the affective current is alive and flowing in every person in the group at all times. Questions such as "What are you feeling at an emotional level?" or "When John says that, how does that make you feel?" or "Will you check in with your feelings right now?" are all basic moves in the GGT therapist's playbook. All of these questions, and many of the leader's interventions, are aimed at lending support to group members who are trying to make contact with their affective current, so that through affective processing it brings group members into better contact with themselves and with each other.

The affective current, of its own accord, does not automatically connect group members with each other. In fact, the affective current will frequently get enacted in ways that can be destructive to the group process if group members are unable to engage in sufficiently effective affective processing. By contrast, affective processing is the very thing that provides the connective tissue between group members. In the common search for meaning in our feelings, we find connection, community, and relationality.

In doing the work of affective processing we discover that there are at least two distinct levels of meaning to be found in the affective current. These are the *signal level* and the *symbolic level*. Let us look at each in turn.

At the signal level, a feeling or bodily sensation provides immediate information about the individual and the field.

> Joe interrupts Mary when she is in the middle of making contact with another group member. Mary feels a rush of anger at Joe for having stepped into her interaction with the other group member.
>
> As a signal, Mary's flash of anger tells her that Joe has encroached on her boundaries and that she needs to set a limit with him.
>
> She asserts herself, saying angrily, "Hey, Joe, stop interrupting me! God, you piss me off!" Joe hears her, blushes, and sheepishly backs off.

Mary has shown healthy self-support. She has perceived her anger as a signal that her boundaries were being crossed, and she mobilized this feeling into action that supported her needs. Joe, however, feels hurt and deflated. At the same time, on another level, the affective current is offering something deeply symbolic. Making deeper contact with the affective current is what we are calling affective processing.

> I [Daisy] say to Mary that I appreciate her self-support in setting this limit with Joe. I ask her about her feelings in having asserted herself in this way. She tells the group and me about her somatic experience of her anger. And this gives rise to a strong memory of her father, whom she experienced as weak and easily hurt. Although he was frequently intrusive with her, she would swallow the anger for fear of hurting him.

Now we are doing the work of affective processing: diving deeper into the waters of the affective current so that we can perceive the affect not just as signal, but also as symbol. The feeling is connected both with the current situation, and with history. When we are diving in the deep waters of symbolizing, there is much potential for connection between group members, because there is so much that we share at the deepest levels.

> I try to grab hold of the potential for connecting in the present moment and see if we can work with the feelings between Mary and Joe. I ask Mary how it felt to set a limit with Joe. She replies, "It felt

good. I've gotten to know that Joe is strong, and that I can be honest with him and he'll be okay." I turn to Joe and ask, "How does it feel that Mary experiences you as strong enough to be honest with?" Joe replies to me, "I like it." Joe turns to Mary, and says, "It feels good that you see my strength, Mary. I want you to let me know when I interrupt you in the future." Now there are smiles of appreciation in the room for both Mary and Joe.

This example illustrates that working with affective processing at the *signal level* enhances group members' empowerment and is a support to the self-activating aspect in guiding our actions (the signal of Mary's anger supports her *limit setting* with Joe). Working at the *symbolic level* brings us to deeper understanding, and connects history with the present moment (finding the deeper connections with her anger supports her *relationship* with Joe). This level of work is a support to the intimately connected self, in that it brings members into a shared experience of exploring at the deepest levels. The signal levels and symbolic levels are complementary, and refer to deeper levels of understanding our affective current, just as the self-activating aspect and the intimately connected aspect are complementary and must both be supported in GGT.[5]

Dialogue around Rupture and Repair of the Selfobject Tie is an Ongoing Process in GGT

Before we focus on the importance of rupture and repair of the selfobject tie in GGT, it may be helpful to review Kohut's (1971) concept of the *selfobject* as it is used in relational gestalt therapy and in self psychology. Lynne Jacobs (1992) states that:

> *Self structure is developed and maintained through "selfobject" ties to other people. The term "selfobject" refers to an object experienced subjectively as serving certain functions ... a dimension of experiencing an object in which a specific bond is required for maintaining, restoring or consolidating the organization of self experience.*
> (cited in Stolorow, Brandchaft, & Atwood, 1987, p. 16)

> *In everyday life, our sense of common purpose with colleagues or neighbors, or even the nation we live in, is a selfobject in that it reinforces our temporal stability and supports a positively toned sense of self-with-other.*
> (ibid, p. 29)

Jacobs's "positively toned sense of self-with-other" provides a basic ground of support for group members in their healing journey in GGT.

When this basic ground of support—the selfobject tie—fails or is threatened for a group member, we refer to this as a *rupture*. The work of reestablishing the selfobject tie we refer to as *repair*.

Walter Stone, a leading group therapy theorist from the field of self psychology, discusses how the therapy group can serve a selfobject function for group members. Stone (2012, p. 108) states:

> *The interpersonal setting of group psychotherapy is particularly suited for patients with deficits to utilize others as selfobjects in the development of a cohesive sense of self. Group members use one another or their inner image of the group-as-a-whole to stabilize their self-esteem and potentially develop more enduring structure and be less vulnerable to narcissistic hurts.*

One further formulation is important in understanding the emotional significance of rupture and repair to the individual group member and for the group-as-a-whole. Stolorow and colleagues (1987) describe a polarity that they call the *repetitive dimension* versus the *selfobject dimension*. In the repetitive dimension, we hold the expectation that our vulnerabilities will be met with the same lack of attunement that they were met with in the original situation, thereby forcing us into fixed gestalts whose origin lies in old patterns of self-protection. At the other end of this polarity is the hope of being held with an attunement that creates enough safety for us to open old wounds to new sources of healing and growth. This dimension Stolorow calls the *selfobject dimension*. Stolorow's powerful formulation helps us understand the stakes and the significance of the process of rupture and repair for the group member. Ruptures that do not get repaired throw the group member into the repetitive dimension, where she must establish safety for herself with fixed gestalts—repetitive routines of self-regulation that may well impede openness and growth. Since the repetitive dimension often involves disturbances in the group member's interpersonal contact-making and boundary regulation, when one group member is thrown into the repetitive dimension others in the group often feel the change in the group field, and they themselves experience difficulty staying open to the selfobject dimension. We have found it useful to teach our groups about the process of rupture and repair in order to identify and normalize the process. Additionally, we have found that teaching about rupture and repair helps to mobilize the insights and perspectives of all group members in identifying and helping to repair ruptures that occur in the group process.

Ruptures of the selfobject tie frequently occur below the level of awareness. This makes sense when we consider that ruptures tend to throw the group member into the repetitive dimension of experience, and the repetitive dimension, as its name implies, is deeply familiar to each person. In unawareness, we are fixedly adapted to living in the repetitive dimension, and the events that invoke this dimension of experience, being part of a well-worn pattern of experiencing, may feel entirely normal to the group member.

> Cheryl was a group member who had played the role of a caregiver whose own needs were neglected in her family of origin. It felt entirely normal to her when she fell into such a role in the group. The "neglected caregiver" was a very familiar stance for her in the repetitive dimension, and therefore a difficult constellation for her to mentalize as it formed in the group. It would be analogous to a fish thinking about the water she swims in—why would she think about that? The water has always been there!
>
> However, in the group, a new set of feelings got stirred up for her when the group attended to her in novel and supportive ways. This attention stirred up Cheryl's hope for a new sense of herself, based on group members' attention to her long-neglected need to be seen and appreciated for her many wonderful qualities—qualities that had nothing to do with caretaking, such as a wicked sense of humor, a lovely sexiness, and an amazing singing voice. This new and as yet fragile sense of herself was a tenuous thread held together by the selfobject tie to the group and its leaders.
>
> One day during group, Cheryl started to talk about a date she went on. This was something new and exciting for her that represented growth supported by her selfobject tie to the group. Another group member spoke about her ill mother. The entire group dropped Cheryl and dealt with the other group member. Cheryl shut down for the rest of the session, but nobody in the group, including us leaders, tuned into her withdrawal. The next week, Cheryl said that she was thinking about leaving the group in order to spend more time doing volunteer work with the homeless. It then dawned on us that Cheryl had perhaps suffered a rupture to the selfobject tie in the previous session. With discussion and careful unpacking, Cheryl was able to gain awareness of what had happened in the previous group and her response to it. The whole group was able to help repair the rupture by taking responsibility for our part in it, and Cheryl was finally able to excitedly share with us the story of her budding new relationship. She stayed on with the group for another two years, finishing when she had grown more fully into a new, fuller sense of herself.

Ruptures experienced below the level of awareness have a tendency to show up in the form of enactments, such as a group member suddenly announcing that she is leaving the group, citing such seemingly innocuous reasons as, "I'm leaving group because I've taken up meditation and have decided to pursue my spiritual development" or "I'm working on taking better care of myself. It's hard for me to get here to the group after a long day at work, and leaving the group is something I'm choosing to do to take better care of myself." We have found that there is often something important left out of such pronouncements, something associated with a rupture in the selfobject tie. Opening up a dialogue into whether the group member has experienced a rupture, perhaps one that has occurred below the level of awareness, can be a fruitful inquiry. Of course, it is incumbent on the GGT leader to honor the group member's autonomous decision about whether to stay in the group, and to treat that decision with respect, but the leader's respect for the member's autonomy is well balanced by the leader's sensitivity to ruptures in the selfobject tie, which may underlie abrupt decisions to leave the group. It is in part for this reason that we generally ask members early on to give four sessions' notice before leaving our groups.

Within an interactive group process, there are many occasions when individual group members will feel dropped, hurt, misunderstood, neglected, overexposed, or mis-met. All of these can create the experience of rupture of the selfobject tie. These hurts may come from other group members, from the group leaders, or from both. In the emotional atmosphere of GGT, it is no wonder that participants are especially vulnerable, for they are working on letting down the usual defenses that protect them from hurt. Furthermore, the value of honesty in the group supports members in articulating feelings of hurt, so that the group can work with ruptures and look at the interactions that have given rise to ruptures from a variety of perspectives. Then all group members can engage in the work of owning responsibility for their piece of the rupture—which then becomes the work of repair. Thus, rupture and repair become an ongoing group process.

Repair refers to reestablishment of the selfobject tie and the restoration of the selfobject dimension of experiencing in the group. The primary methods of fostering repair in the group process are:

1. Slowing down
2. Unpacking
3. Searching for positive intention
4. Restoring the empathic link

Looking more closely at the process of rupture and repair in the context of the group process we discover that there are innumerable ways in which these ruptures may occur. Below are a few common patterns of interaction that can get enacted in the group process, giving rise to an experience of rupture. This list is by no means exhaustive—we share it simply to illustrate the kinds of occurrence that can cause a rupture of the selfobject tie:

Being dropped—A group member shares something that feels important to them, and the group prematurely moves on to another issue.

Being interpreted—A group member feels that they have been put into an interpretive box by the leader or another member.

Being overexposed—A group member has revealed more than they are comfortable with and feel ashamed.

Being ignored—A group member is left alone by the group and feels insignificant or invisible.

Being coerced—A group member feels that the group is pressuring them to do something for which they are not ready.

Being overprotected—A group member feels that the leader or other members come in and save them, thereby limiting their opportunity to risk.

In reading this list, you may recognize that these occurrences cannot be completely avoided. For instance, it is just about impossible to have a group process in which members are free from feeling dropped every now and then. In truth, all of these occurrences are part of the normal interactive flow of a lively group process. Therefore, our goal in GGT is to work with these issues as they occur, rather than to strive for a utopian group experience in which no one ever gets hurt. This is where rupture and repair become vital processes requiring special skills. When the group appreciates that the experience of rupture provides the entire group with an opportunity to learn and grow, then the group normalizes the process of creating dialogue around these issues. It is the dialogue about the rupture that opens up the possibility of repair.

Repair involves the process of listening to the member who feels hurt, taking in how the hurtful events felt to him, and honoring his narrative of the hurtful interactions. Further, repair involves the process of each of the people involved taking responsibility for the part they played in the hurtful interaction. Repair also involves the person who has been hurt listening to other group members' feelings and their narrative of events. Repair is a deeply interpersonal exploration. It is a journey of listening, empathy, pain-tolerance, responsibility-taking, open-mindedness, and open-heartedness on the part of the person who feels hurt, those who participated in the events, the leader, and ultimately all group members, as every member of the group field has an effect on all group events.

Some of the most important work of healing in GGT occurs in the processes of dialogue around rupture and repair. In the process of creating dialogue around rupture and repair, group members learn a great deal about empathy, patience, working through difficulty, tolerating the pain of anxiety and shame, commitment, and taking responsibility. Relationships among group members are frequently strengthened in these dialogues.

The work of rupture and repair lies at the heart of relational development. Just as an individual's capacity for reflecting on and working through her psychic wounds defines to a large extent her capacity for richly relational living, so too does the gestalt group's facility in sustaining dialogue about rupture and repair largely define the group's capacity for relationality. Much of the healing in GGT derives from working through the difficulties that arise during group interactions. Therefore, we seek a culture in GGT that has, as a major value, group members' willingness to come forward with the hurts they have experienced in the group process, so that the group will have the opportunity for the growth that the ensuing dialogue and contact about rupture and repair provides.

Conclusion

Participating in gestalt groups over the years has been like a grand journey in a caravan peopled with seekers of truth, authenticity, and connection. Participants in GGT come together, knowing that what we seek is at least as much about the journey as it is about the destination. In this chapter we have sought to capture some of the insights, experiences, and musings that have animated our thinking up to this point as we continue on the journey.

Our experience has shown us that GGT provides a powerful milieu for growth that is grounded in the relational. We have found that, when effectively facilitated, a culture can evolve in the gestalt group that is safe enough to do life's riskiest and most rewarding work: opening up, sharing our secrets, showing our strengths and vulnerabilities, learning how to become more honest, more compassionate, more present, and more connected to others. We have found that the group environment supports its members in becoming more fully integrated people who frequently develop in significant ways as a result of their group involvement.

Notes

1 An earlier version of this chapter first appeared as an article in 2013 in *GROUP: The Journal of the Eastern Group Psychotherapy Society* (37(3), 185–218).

2 The authors wish to thank Lee Kassan, MA, for his patience, guidance, and editorial excellence in helping us shape this chapter through many drafts. We

also thank Bud Feder, PhD, for his careful and astute feedback on an earlier draft of this chapter.

3 Justin Hecht's (2011) discussion of the transcendent function in solving the problem of the opposites, a complementary formulation from the Jungian tradition, was a great help in developing these ideas.

4 Barbara Stevens Sullivan's (2009) discussion of Bion's concept of beta and alpha elements was helpful in developing this section, and many of the ideas in this article. We highly recommend her book, *The Mystery of Analytical Work: Weavings from Jung and Bion* (Routledge, 2009), to psychotherapists of all persuasions.

5 See Cole (1998) for a more in-depth look at affect as signal and symbol.

References

Aylward, J. (1996). An extended group experience. In B. Feder & R. Ronall (Eds), *A living legacy of Fritz and Laura Perls: Contemporary case studies* (pp. 235 251). New Orleans, LA: Gestalt Institute Press.

Beisser, A. (1971). Paradoxical theory of change. In J. Fagan & I. L. Shepherd (Eds), *Gestalt therapy now* (pp. 77–80). New York: Harper Colophon.

Bion, W. R. (1960). *Experiences in groups*. New York: Basic Books.

Bloom, D. (2008). In pursuit of gestalt therapy group process: Group process as self process. In B. Feder & J. Frew (Eds), *Beyond the hot seat revisited: Gestalt approaches to group* (pp. 53–66). New Orleans, LA: Gestalt Institute Press.

Cole, P. (1998). Affective process in psychotherapy: A gestalt therapist's view. *Gestalt Journal, 21*(1), 49–72.

Fairfield, M. (2009). Dialogue in complex systems: The hermeneutical attitude. In L. Jacobs & R. Hycner (Eds), *Relational approaches in gestalt therapy* (pp. 193–220). Santa Cruz, CA: GestaltPress.

Feder, B. (2006). *Gestalt group therapy: A practical guide*. New Orleans, LA: Gestalt Institute Press.

Feder, B., & Ronall, R. (Eds) (1980). *Beyond the hot seat: Gestalt approaches to group*. New Orleans, LA: Gestalt Institute Press.

Hecht, J. (2011). Becoming who we are in groups: One Jungian's approach to group psychotherapy. *Group, 35*(2), 151–165.

Hycner, R. (1993). *Between person and person: Toward a dialogical psychotherapy*. Highland, NY: Gestalt Journal Press.

Jacobs, L. (1992). Insights from psychoanalytic self psychology and intersubjectivity theory for gestalt therapists. *Gestalt Journal, 15*(2), 25–60.

Jacobs, L., & Hycner, R. (1995). *The healing relationship in gestalt therapy: A dialogic/self psychology approach*. Highland, NY: Gestalt Journal Press.

Kepner, E. (1980). Gestalt group process. In B. Feder & R. Ronall (Eds), *Beyond the hot seat: Gestalt approaches to group* (pp. 5–24). New York: Brunner/Mazel.

Kohut, H. (1971). *The analysis of the self*. New York: International Universities Press.

Perls, F. S. (1973). *The gestalt approach and eyewitness to therapy*. New York: Bantam Books.

Perls, F. S., Hefferline, R., & Goodman, P. (1951). *Gestalt therapy: Excitement and growth in the human personality.* New York: Julian Press.

Philippson, P. (2009). *The emergent self: An existential-gestalt approach.* London: Karnac Books.

Polster, E. (1995). *A population of selves: A therapeutic exploration of personal diversity.* San Francisco, CA: Jossey-Bass.

Resnick, R. (1978). Chicken soup is poison. In F. Stephenson (Ed.), *Gestalt therapy primer* (pp. 142–146). New York: Aronson.

Rutan, J. S., Stone, W., & Shay, J. (2007). *Psychodynamic group psychotherapy,* 4th edition. New York: Guilford Press.

Simkin, J. (1998). *Gestalt therapy mini-lectures.* Gouldsboro, ME: Gestalt Journal Press.

Staemmler, F.-M. (2009). *Aggression, time, and understanding: Contributions to the evolution of gestalt therapy.* New York: GestaltPress/Routledge.

Stolorow, R., Brandchaft, B., & Atwood, G. (1987). *Psychoanalytic treatment: An intersubjective approach.* Hillsdale, NJ: Analytic Press.

Stone, W. (2012). The curative fantasy as a protective function in group psychotherapy. In I. Harwood, W. Stone, & M. Pines (Eds), *Self experiences in group revisited: Affective attachments, intersubjective regulations and human understanding* (pp. 107–118). New York: Routledge.

Sullivan, B. S. (2009). *The mystery of analytical work: Weavings from Jung and Bion.* New York: Routledge.

Wheeler, G. (2000). *Beyond individualism: Toward an understanding of self, relationship, and experience.* Cambridge, MA: Gestalt Institute of Cleveland Press.

Yalom, I. D. (1995). *The theory and practice of group psychotherapy,* 4th edition. New York: Basic Books.

Yontef, G. M. (1993). *Awareness, dialogue and process: Essays on Gestalt therapy.* Gouldsboro, ME: Gestalt Journal Press.

Zinker, J. (1977). *Creative process in gestalt therapy.* New York: Brunner/Mazel.

Zinker, J. (1998). *In search of good form: Gestalt therapy with couples and families.* New York: Taylor & Francis.

Žižek, S. (2011). *Living in the end times.* London: Verso.

Chapter 3

In the Presence of the Sacred

This chapter is written in Daisy's voice

Joy is the appreciation of beauty.

—Dick Olney

... you and I, and I and Thou
Are more than deadly matter;
Participating, we exist
In truly Buddha nature.

—Fritz Perls

The circle of chairs is ready and gradually the group begins to gather. The feeling in the air contains an equal mix of excitement and anxiety. Long-time members greet each other with affectionate familiarity, while newer members enter more quietly and find a seat. A candle is lit and the group begins.

In this chapter we try to capture something ineffable and extraordinary about gestalt group therapy: its sacredness and its beauty. Erv Polster (2006, p. 21) captures the shift in awareness that occurs when group members enter into the atmosphere of the group:

> *Before the group therapy session would begin, people would converse in normal terms; call these conversations secular. Just ordinary conversation took place; bright and lively. Then at some point, when the time to start the session arrived, I would say, "Let's start." This put an end to that lively conversation! I had unwittingly implied a new form of conversation, not anywhere evident in the previous one. The implication was that from now on every word would count. There was a new opening to heightened awareness of both self and the others in the group, one that raised the ante as people entered their personal expressions into the group pot.*

It is sacred work that we're engaged in. This is a sacredness that is human, or as Martin Buber might say: *inter-human*. We touch something that has a gentle, elusive beauty when group members become deeply connected. We can sense it, almost like a faint whiff of incense in the room. What are the elements of that sacred connection?

As we discussed in Chapter 2, a safe and strong container is key to relational development. It is also a key to the evocation of the sacred. Group members risk the vulnerability of being seen in their emotional nakedness. Old hurts, shameful secrets, needs, and fears that can feel too vulnerable for words are brought into the group. Tender and profound relationships develop among and between members and leaders. GGT members have opportunities to see and be seen by one another in ways that many of them have only rarely, if ever, experienced. Learning how to nurture these bonds with sensitivity, while at the same time making room for honest and authentic feedback, is a large part of the work of GGT, and this juxtaposition of vulnerability and honesty seems to be key to evoking that elusive quality we refer to as sacred connection.

Another vital aspect of "sacred connection" in GGT is the art of "holding the potential." This work is done primarily by the leader in a newly developing group, but increasingly by the members over time. Holding the potential refers to the work of seeing possibilities for a person that the group member may have little or no sense of yet. Holding the potential does not mean foisting another's (either the leader's or another member's) idea of "what is best" for the person; rather, it involves catching glimmers of qualities that have gone underdeveloped—grace, humor, wisdom, ambition, self-acceptance—affirming and nurturing these qualities. In effect, the group as a whole says to the individual group member, "We will hold these aspects of yours until you're ready to claim them for yourself."

Erv Polster discusses the group as a "Thou" in an "I–Thou" relationship with each group member. In this sense, the group-as-a-whole becomes a holding environment for each group member. Polster (2015, p. 160) observes how the group can:

> derive great leverage as a quasi-personhood from its relational importance to its members. The group develops a character of its own by the way the members dialogue with it, within it, and about it. They think about the group, they talk to the group, they visualize the group, they belong to the group. Everyone knows that the group, at bottom, is a collection of individual people. It has no other concrete actuality. Still, it has a special psychological existence, an anthropomorphic image offering continuity, cohesion, personality, and purpose. The group is responsive, it is supervisory, it is stimulating, it creates the feeling of belonging. It takes on the qualities of a supra

individual. The only voice it has is through the aggregate of people who comprise it, relate to it, honor it, and love it. In this sense it is an enlarged person.

Polster shows here how group itself can become the "other" who sees and holds each group member. This quality of being held and seen can evoke a sense of the sacred, rendering all that occurs in the group significant and meaningful.

In the case vignette below, we discuss two deeply human situations that arose in GGT in which that elusive feeling of the sacred emerged. In the first vignette, we see how the group held a group member even when there was little hope for improvement of her condition, yet a kind of emotional or even existential healing occurred for her and the group in the process of holding that connection. In the second vignette, we see how the group can serve as a container for dialogue in helping members to connect and work through relational ruptures.

To Bear with Unbearable Sorrow: The Story of Mary

As we discussed earlier, one of the sacred components of group work is the establishment of a container strong and safe enough to hold feelings of every kind. Probably the most difficult and painful feeling for a group to hold is one of grief around irreparable loss. Sometimes a person reaches a point in her life when it is clear that things simply cannot get much better. She may be in physical decline or she may be carrying such a heavy history of deprivation and abuse that embracing the future feels impossible.

In Mary's case, both of these things were true. At 65, she was underweight and prematurely frail, with numerous health conditions. Walking was difficult for her and she was in near-constant pain from arthritis. Her husband's physical and emotional condition was worse than hers and he needed a great deal of Mary's attention. Mary had a childhood history of abuse and neglect and, sadly, the pain had been passed down the generations. Mary's son and adult granddaughter were struggling with addiction.

Not surprisingly, Mary's energy in the group was very limited. She often sat on the corner of the couch and frequently fell fast asleep. She'd sit, snoring quietly, until a group member poked her or raised voices jolted her awake.

So—how did the group feel about Mary? They loved her! Group members often referred to her as their "anchor," and she did, indeed, offer a grounding, consoling presence to group members struggling or in distress. She had grandchildren, and people would sometimes say they pictured themselves being held on Mary's lap the same way she would hold the grandchildren. Yes, the group loved Mary and the feeling was certainly mutual. She could no longer drive, and she traveled by para-transit to the group sessions, which often took several hours, yet she hardly ever missed a session.

Though the group was quite familiar with Mary's current life situation, she had only rarely talked about her childhood. Then during one group session, the dam burst. Mary started telling the story of her early life. One of nine children, growing up in rural Arkansas, with an alcoholic father and a mother who raged—screaming abuse and dealing out physical blows on a daily basis—Mary learned early to protect herself by running and often hiding in the tool shed. Many nights, she told us, she would find herself locked out of the house and would spend the night sleeping in the shed. Amid the chaos, it's not surprising that Mary and her sisters were the victims of sexual abuse as well as neglect and physical abuse. As trauma piled upon trauma, Mary comforted herself with food, and often begged from neighboring families or stole from the corner store. Soon compulsive eating and bulimia added to her distress.

It was a dark November evening when Mary's story came pouring forth. No one said a word as she was talking and sobbing. When she had finished, the group sat in stunned silence. Of course, the group had worked with many stories of distressing situations and dysfunctional families, but somehow this seemed different. The extent of Mary's past trauma, her current suffering, and her willingness to be vulnerable in the group combined to create an extraordinarily poignant scene. As the group came to a close, the members formed a circle around Mary and, as she nodded her permission, wrapped her in the gentlest of embraces.

Following this experience, Mary's commitment to the group and theirs to her was solidified. She continued the laborious process of taking para-transit, and she reached out with sensitivity to every member of the group.

When Mary's husband called to tell us that she had become too ill to attend group, members sent cards and flowers to her home. They pooled cash to help pay for a specially designed wheelchair. Most importantly, they held her lovingly in their hearts.

There was certainly no "cure" for Mary, and her external reality only worsened as her health rapidly declined with a worsening lung condition. It did seem, though, that even as her body experienced inexorable entropy, Mary herself had an experience of profound healing. People she loved had looked at her "worst" with her and been able to hold it without turning away. The group demonstrated that nothing is unbearable when we are held in the presence of a loving other.

The Joy and Pain of Developing Authentic Relationships: Pamela and Mark

The Wednesday evening group was scheduled to begin at 7:00 p.m. Around 5:30 p.m., an email arrived from Pamela: "I won't be at the group today. Please let everyone know that I'm considering not returning."

What? For four years Pamela had been a reliable, well-loved member of the group. Peter and I had often commented on how significantly she'd grown and changed over those years. Clearly, a conflict that had occurred in the previous session between Pamela and Mark, another group member, had been far more painful for Pamela than we had appreciated. We immediately called Pamela, and, with some urging, were able to convince her to come to group that evening.

To make this more understandable, it's helpful to know a bit about Pamela's history.

A sensitive, deeply thoughtful child, Pamela had been raised in a prosperous, cool, "arm's length" family. Her parents were both chemists who worked in private industry. Although everything was provided for her, little affection or intimacy was expressed in her family. As an artistic and highly emotionally attuned girl, Pamela's family looked at her like a "stranger in a strange land" when she expressed a range of feelings beyond cool rationality. Moreover, as the sole holder of the family's emotions, she felt all the anger, sadness, and other emotions that other family members denied, and thereby became the family's "identified patient." When Pamela discovered gestalt work as an adult, she was thrilled to find a place where her emotional life was valued and she could express herself without fear of being seen as an outsider for paying attention to and expressing her feelings. She works as a set designer for a prestigious repertory theater.

Pamela had developed a close relationship with a number of people in the group, including Mark. Mark's history was the polar opposite of Pamela's. He grew up poor, with a violent father and a passive, beaten-down mother. There were very few resources available—either emotionally or financially. After serving in the military, Mark availed himself of veterans' educational benefits, was the first in his family to go off to college, and eventually became an electrical engineer, pulling in a sizeable income and living in an elegant house on the river. After his chaotic and violent childhood, enjoying a peaceful, nourishing life felt important to him. He was often quiet in group. He enjoyed the support of the group, but it was difficult for him to share his feelings.

In the previous group session, Pamela had shared her feelings toward Mark—that he was not forthcoming enough in group. She felt strongly that the purpose of group was for each of us to share our feelings. Mark said that, for him, sometimes it was best just to be with the group, and that sharing his feelings was often too exhausting. When Pamela persisted in her request that Mark be more forthcoming, a flash of Mark's short-tempered father came out in his interaction with Pamela—he told her to "back off, leave me alone, and stop pulling at me."

Pamela was devastated by Mark's reaction. It felt to her like a replay of her family in which she was ridiculed and rejected for speaking to the feelings in her family. For his part, Mark felt annoyed that Pamela seemed to have an agenda for how he was to act in group; she wanted him to express his feelings. But for Mark, being in group that way was not what he wanted or needed. They had ended the previous group with tension between them.

At the next group, Pamela, angry and hurt, confronted us, saying,

> I don't want to be part of a group where everything's on the surface. I thought this was a place where people talked about their feelings! And when Mark shut me down like that, I realized that this group is not a place where I can do my work.

It was at this point that several group members entered into the mix to really hold both Pamela and Mark. They were able to see that both Mark and Pamela's early wounding had gotten triggered in their previous exchange. It felt to Mark like his need to be quietly nourished by the group after a childhood filled with trauma was not okay. At the same time, it felt to Pamela that her need to be in an honest and emotionally expressive environment was not being respected or understood in the group. A number of group members (with a little help from us group leaders) were able to support both Mark and Pamela with the rupture that had occurred between them.

With enough group support, Mark was able to address the situation in a way that allowed some healing to begin:

> You know I appreciate you, Pamela, and I love the way you're tuned in to my feelings. But you have to understand—emotional talk can be incredibly intense for me and I'm not always up to it. I was never able to just relax and be myself as a kid. It was walking on eggshells to keep my dad from exploding, and being like a husband to my mom to try to get her out of her depression. I've got a big "love deficit" that I'm trying to fill, and just being in the group, kind of soaking it in, feels good to me. I'm hoping you can appreciate that and be okay with it. I'm okay to talk about feelings in here, but sometimes I need you to be okay with me being quiet in here.

Pamela, rather sheepishly, nodded and smiled. She responded,

> Yeah, I know I can go a little over the top. I think I understand you better. But can you see also what I need? I can't be in a place where nobody talks about anything—that's what I grew up with, and I can't do that anymore.

Mark replied,

> Yes, I get that Pamela. I understand where you're coming from. I support you getting that.

Pamela looked relieved and gratified when she simply said, "Thank you Mark." The group released its collective breath as Pamela and Mark embraced.

When a rupture between group members is worked through, and group members are able to work their way past reactivity and defensiveness to find their way again to each other's open, vulnerable heart, it feels that something good has happened. That "something good" often has the fleeting fragrance of the sacred—an elusive quality that seems to say: healing can occur; people can connect; together we can attend to the beauty that surrounds us.

The presence of the sacred in GGT ultimately involves the group serving as witness to the emotional growth of each of its members. Each GGT member is both witness to and participant in a growth process that involves emotional risk and vulnerability. When group members are successfully facilitated in the establishment of an atmosphere of risking, growing, and healing together, then graceful moments of the sacred may arrive like an unexpected visitor.

References

Olney, R. (1990). Personal interview at workshop in Berkeley, CA, August 10.

Perls, F. S. (1969). *In and out of the garbage pail*. Lafayette, CA: Real People Press.

Polster, E. (2006). *Uncommon ground: Harmonizing psychotherapy and community to enhance everyday living*. Phoenix, AZ: Zeig, Tucker & Theisen.

Polster, E. (2015). *Beyond therapy: Igniting life focus community movements*. Piscataway, NJ: Transaction Publishers.

Chapter 4

In the Shadow of the Leader
Power, Reflection, and Dialogue in Gestalt Group Therapy

This chapter is written in Peter's voice

In this chapter[1] we seek to shed light on the relationship between the leader and members in gestalt group therapy. We hope to provide a perspective that will help gestalt group leaders to better understand and navigate difficulties and complexities that arise in this relationship.

Vulnerabilities run high in GGT where the felt potential for healing and growth exists along with a corresponding felt danger of the potential for wounding and shame.[2] The membership and leadership[3] of the group co-create an intersubjective field that is rich in complexity, always in process, always unfolding and never fully understood by any group participant, member, or leader. When negative or shaming experiences arise, insight and intelligence concerning the difficulty and its resolution are distributed among the group's membership and leadership, with each person holding a valuable perspective.

We will refer to the relationship between the leader and the members as the leadership/membership field. The leadership/membership field has a special role in this process orientation to GGT. Reflection and dialogue around the experience of the leadership/membership field provide a rich ground of inquiry in which members have the opportunity to work with fundamental feelings toward self and other and fundamental modes of self-organization. Members are held by the leadership with support and connectedness to explore feelings toward the leadership; these feelings may be sharply drawn or amorphous, positive or negative. With the support of the leadership, group members explore their ongoing, unfolding affective responses to the leadership and discover much about themselves in the process.

The leader, herself human and far from all-knowing, brings her own vulnerabilities, blind spots, misapprehensions, and desires into the leadership/membership field. We have come to designate the process whereby the membership's feelings meet the leader's vulnerabilities—"the shadow of the leader." When the leader "gets" that her vulnerabilities are okay, and that part of her "good-enough" leadership is to accept her humanness and to encourage dialogue, then she can support the group in dialogues on the shadow of the leader. In our experience, these dialogues can potentiate growth and development for each individual member, for the group as a whole, and for the leader.

Vignette I: Rupture and Repair in the Leadership/ Membership Field

In a gestalt group for therapists that we facilitated several years ago, Rita was a new member who entered the group process with much energy. She shared frequently and passionately about issues regarding her challenges at work and her husband's health difficulties—issues that evoked sympathy in group members but lacked a depth of self-reflection. After a number of group meetings, we shared with our clinical consultant a growing perception that Rita was not leaving enough space for others to talk. Rita's thoughts followed one after another without sufficient time for either the leaders or other members to share. We had tried to wait her out, to let her pick up on more subtle cues, all to no avail. It began to dawn on us that we had to intervene, and we determined to do so with a minimum of shame.

At the next session, Rita started in at the very first opportunity, bringing in another health challenge that her husband was facing. Yet again she left little space for others, and group members appeared to be sympathetic yet growing tired of her dominance of group time.

Intervening in this artfully was not easy, and we proceeded the best we could. When Rita left a very short pause, I asked if others had ever felt similarly to Rita. Rita was not happy with this interruption, and said to me with much agitation, "Peter, are you aware that I was not finished?" This was the opening of a very charged and rich dialogue. Daisy and I shared with Rita that indeed we did know that she was not finished, but that we wished to help her participate in the group while leaving space for others' participation. I did a piece of work with Rita around this in the group, which was intense for both of us but seemed to me to come to a fair place of resolution by the end of the session.

The following session, Rita shared that she had felt deeply shamed by Daisy and me in the preceding session and that she was planning to leave the group. We shared with Rita our appreciation for her courage in coming back and talking about her negative reactions to us. She said that she had been dreading coming back to the group earlier in the week, had experienced difficulty sleeping and concentrating over the week, and had discussed with her husband the notion of leaving the group. Part of her felt that the entire group would scold and shame her, yet she held out some hope that the group might respond with support. I offered a "group-as-a-whole" perspective at this point that Rita was leading the way for members to talk about their negative reactions to Daisy and me. This perspective seemed to lend Rita confidence, at which point she shared a perception of me as remote and cold and Daisy as intrusive. Daisy and I supported Rita in giving voice to her perceptions of us, and asked if other group members felt similarly to her, inviting others to join her, so that she would not be isolated in her negative feelings toward us and to protect her from being scapegoated in holding critical perceptions of the leaders[4] (Alonso, 1993; Agazarian, 2004; Beck, 1981; Wheeler & Jones 2003).

Other members joined in with offering critical perceptions of us, which we listened to with great interest, knowing that in this smart and perceptive group, we had much to learn about ourselves. We listened and shared our "here and now" responses to the feedback. We tried to neither become defensive (which would deflect contact) nor enter into our own emotional/psychological work in the group (and thereby abandon our leadership role—so vital for the safety of the group). We shared our appreciation of the group's courage, along with excitement for a new level of honesty and risk-taking emerging as the group confronted us. We talked openly in the group about our own individual and group consultation (we feel this is important modeling in a therapy group for therapists). In sharing our here-and-now emotional responses, we also talked explicitly about the boundaries we respect when we are in the "leaders' chairs." We let the group know that we were open to hearing any and all feedback, and that we would work with particularly difficult or triggering feedback in our own therapy and clinical consultation.

A sense of trust and holding started to form in the session, laying the ground for Rita to go to a far more vulnerable place in sharing about terrible physical and emotional abuse she had suffered as a child, and how our earlier intervention triggered many deeply traumatic memories. Now Rita began to let the group nurture her, and she began to notice how leaving more space provided greater opportunity for her to receive the good feelings the group had to offer her. She left space for others to share, and found deep connection with another group member who had found enough safety in Rita's new-found vulnerability in the group to share her own experiences of early trauma. Rita had finally learned how to share time and space in the group. She decided to continue with the group, and we all grew a little bit that session.

Normalizing Tensions in the Leadership/Membership Field

The leadership/membership field is composed of the relationship between the group members and the leader. When the leader has a framework for normalizing tensions and conflicts that arise in the leadership/membership field, she is better equipped to stay open and facilitate dialogue on group issues that involve her mis-attunements and shortcomings, or simply hurts that occur in the discharging of her responsibilities of leadership. These discussions are rarely easy for the leader, yet they can be richly rewarding when approached with openness.

Enactment

The plot thickens considerably when the leader's personal issues intersect with vulnerabilities of group members. It is our experience that, just as in marriages, where vulnerabilities and wounds often cross-fertilize, so it is in groups that the vulnerabilities of the leader have a way of showing up, meeting up with the vulnerabilities of the group members, and getting enacted. These enactments can emerge in a great many ways.

Vignette 2: Enactment in the Leadership/ Membership Field

Over 25 years ago, when I was in the middle of a painful divorce, I was "stuck" with my therapist group. Members were coming forward and working on their personal issues, work that was valid and important in its own way, yet contact between group members was superficial. Members were not being real with each other, nor did they bring up their negative feelings toward me. The group lacked vitality. In consultation it became clear that I was much more mired in my personal issues than I was aware of; I was deeply burdened with guilt, anxiety, grief, and loss. This group of young therapists was composed of members who were struggling to find their voice, find their power. Their difficulties with aggression and my vulnerable state of mind coalesced to create a group enactment in which group members treated me and each other with superficiality and a saccharine sweetness that left the group disempowered and passionless. Coming to grips with the ways in which my vulnerabilities were intersecting with the group's issues was a source of both suffering and growth.

I addressed the issue with the group, inviting their perceptions of me and how I was running the group. A few brave members talked about feeling that I was fragile and about not wanting to rock the boat in the group. I worked with these issues in my consultation and therapy. Once the group could talk about these feelings, the energy in the group picked up; group members felt more comfortable challenging me and each other, and we worked through this enactment. But it did not come easily for me or for the group members. We could now meet each other more fully and work with feelings such as competition and attraction—feelings that added new vitality, sexuality, and excitement to the process and brought the group to life (Aledort, 2009).

Fulfilling the Leadership Role while Maintaining the Dialogic Stance

The leader has a job to do, with many responsibilities to the membership, the most important of which is to create a safe-enough space for the group to do its work (Feder, 2006). The leader cannot fulfill this responsibility to the group if she is in the middle of doing her own deep emotional work. In order to fulfill this responsibility, this unique role within the group, the leader maintains a dialogic stance while maintaining her vital role of leadership. This inevitably is a balancing act, particularly when conflict and negative feelings arise for members in the leadership/membership field.

In GGT the relationship between the leader and members is an I–Thou, dialogic relationship. The leader is right there in the group, with her authentic self fully engaged. However, she is engaged from the vantage point of the leader. When she takes on the mantle of leadership, she has signed on to make the group members her priority, and to do her own psychological growth work elsewhere. Finding equilibrium between being emotionally present as the leader and maintaining appropriate boundaries is always challenging. One way that we think about this balancing act is to be present to here-and-now responses, but if I as a leader feel that my own deeply seated personal work is getting triggered, then I seek the help of my own therapist and consultants.

Vignette 3: The Leader Abandons His Role

Early in my career, I was leading a men's group. I was full of gestalt therapy idealism at the time, and believed strongly in its egalitarian ethos (but did not yet appreciate its nuances and complexities). One of the group members confronted me on the fact that everyone in the group talked about his personal issues but me, and he challenged me to come down off my "high horse" and bring my issues to the group. He felt that there was no reason that special rules should apply to me just because I was the group leader.

Naively, I took up his challenge. In the following group, I brought up a personal issue, thinking that I could do so and simply resume my leadership role when I was done. Of course, this was not to be the case. Sharing my issue led to intense feelings, memories, and a somatic state that left me in poor condition to continue facilitating the group. It was only with great force of will that I was able to resume my role as group leader.

Discussing the issue later with my consultant, she helped me to consider my needs and self-support as the group leader. What boundaries helped me to function well in the leadership role? How could I take good care of myself in the group?

I went back to the group the next week and told them both about my experience in the prior session and my consultation. I explained that, in order to bring the group the best of my leadership abilities, I could not do my own work there. That men's group stayed together for 15 years. The group members went through much together, and the group was a strong support in their lives. I believe that the group would not have survived and thrived all these years had I not set this important boundary.

The Shadow of the Leader

A holistic view of the leader must include the leader's vulnerabilities, characteristic blind spots, desires, ambitions, and fears. The *shadow of the leader* is composed of the aspects of those vulnerabilities that are out of awareness for the leader within the field of the group. No matter how much work we have done on ourselves, we gestalt group leaders will never transcend our humanness, nor would we want to, for gestalt therapy teaches us to embrace our humanity —to welcome it, not to master it—as mastery of what is within us would amount to a reification of the self. Moreover, each group comprises a new field that will create new blind spots for the leader. The gestalt model teaches us to be curious, to do what we can to stay in contact with the many selves we contain (Polster, 1995). The shadow of the leader is a moving target, co-created by leader and group. Fear, ambition, seduction, humiliation, and all the other horsemen of the human condition will find their way into the gestalt group and will be enacted in some way that involves the leadership. The shadow by no means defines the entirety of the group experience, but when unaddressed will tend to get acted out in ways deleterious to the group and its members. There is no transcendence of the human condition—certainly not for those of us who are engaged in the gloriously mucky work of gestalt group leadership. It is the attitude of the leadership toward the shadow that will determine its effect on the group. If the attitude is one of curiosity and the courage to consider these unsettling dimensions, then the leader models an attitude that will assist the group in its development and help group members stay alive to personal and professional paths of growth and discovery.

A Field Perspective on the Shadow

As I write this, I am sitting on a train. Looking out the window, I see the shadow of the train. It is dynamic. The position of the sun, the movement of the train, the terrain upon which the shadow falls—all of these components create the unfolding dynamic present moment of the train's shadow. So it is with the shadow of the leader. The composition of the group, its stage of development, the person who is sitting in the leader's chair, the attractions and reactions of the leader to group members—all are present in the co-creation of the shadow. No group leader can be aware of all of this experience. All group leaders must necessarily hold some aspects of the field out of awareness in order to focus on other dimensions of the field. The shadow of the leader is always shifting, is field dependent, and is co-created by all the people in the group who comprise the field. It would be impossible for the group leader to be aware of all the dimensions of her response to the almost infinite workings of the group. Instead, the group leader must relax into an attitude of acceptance of not knowing, accompanied by a continual openness to new, surprising meanings that unfold as the group and leader do the work of the group.

The Shadow Reminds Us of Our Humanity and Vulnerability

Wouldn't it be nice if we could arrive at invulnerability? To never be humiliated, to always know where we stand, to know ourselves thoroughly and to be the master of our own responses? Many are the gestalt group leaders with this fantasy. In truth, though, yesterday's most exalted awarenesses may well be today's deflections. The most brilliant moment may have unforeseen and hurtful meanings. As the Polsters (1974) remind us, gestalt therapy is a continual unfolding of polarities. A beautiful piece of work done in the gestalt group may well evoke meaning for a group member that is seemingly quite the opposite of the positive meaning the leader has assigned to it.

We do well to remain curious about and to make space for group members to express the shadow side, even when we are basking in the glow of our most brilliant work. The question, then, is not if the leader has missed, hurt, seduced, been misguided about or dropped group members. Instead, it is a question of how these shadow phenomena have manifested. The gestalt superman who casts no shadow is a bad dream. What a relief it is to know that we will fail, and in accepting our failure we succeed; or to put it differently, it can be a relief to know that all experience casts both light and shadow. All experience has a shadow side, and in accepting this truth, we learn to work with the shadow rather than deny its existence.

Power, Egalitarianism, and the Shadow of the Leader

From the moment that the gestalt group leader forms the group to the last minute of the last meeting of the group, the leader assumes a unique position of power within it. She has the power to guide, intercede, and decide who is admitted into the group. The group meeting typically (but not always) occurs at the leader's office, and the leader is (usually) paid by the group members. In gestalt therapy we bring a democratic, egalitarian sensibility to the psychotherapeutic enterprise with an emphasis on contact as opposed to interpretation as the principal medium by which we do the work of psychotherapy. However, in the gestalt group we sometimes experience an Orwellian sleight of hand in which all the members are equal, but the leader is more equal than others. How we move gestalt group theory forward to bring the gestalt therapy ethos of a more egalitarian therapeutic relationship into being is central to a dialogue around the shadow of the leader. The problem here is the gestalt group leader who wields great power but denies the group the space and permission to discuss her power because her egalitarian self-concept would have it that she holds no special power in the group. How can the group discuss, process, and make contact with the leader's uses and misuses of power if she suffers from an illusion that a differential in power does not exist?

The gestalt group promotes a culture in which members may make new contact, think new thoughts, and articulate as yet unknown aspects of self in the field. Exploration of group members' responses to others and to the leader are essential ingredients of gestalt group process. The gestalt group leader's acceptance of group members' responses to her helps make the group a safer, more egalitarian place. While not all members have the same power as the leader, each has the power of their own perceptions and responses. Each member has their own voice. Creating a group culture that gives permission, support, and validation to members' various responses to the leader helps to equalize power, and helps group members better orient themselves to the field.

Vignette 4: The Leader's Boundary Confusion Causes a Rupture

In a recent group, Bruce, a long-time member, looked very uncomfortable, and I thought it might have something to do with me. I inquired about what was going on, and he told me that he was very angry with me about a message I had sent to the group after the Trump election in the US. I had sent an email saying essentially that group members may well be upset and that the group is here as a support. I had thought that Bruce, as a gay person of color, would have felt supported by my email, but he did not. He felt it inappropriate and manipulative for me to have sent the email out. I was surprised at first, but felt it important to hear all that he was willing to say. Others in the group lent support to him, and joined with their own feelings about my email. When I felt that I had practiced inclusion, had deeply listened, and practiced confirmation—letting him know what I heard and felt from him, then I practiced presence by speaking from my experience and taking responsibility. I told him and the group that, on reflection, I had been deeply dysregulated and put into a state of trauma on election night. My email to the group had been couched in my reaching out *to* them, but underneath I was also reaching out *for* them, in my need for reassurance and connection. Thus, I connected with the needs I had been projecting onto group members— needs for reassurance and connection. With this contact, Bruce and I were able to reconnect.

This vignette illustrates that events in the group have more than one meaning. In fact, any significant group event can have many meanings. While my conscious intent in sending this email was to provide a reminder to group members that they have a safe space in the group to process their feelings about the election, I wrote it on a morning when I was extremely upset and dysregulated. Although it is true that I wanted to share reassuring words, at the same time, and on another level, I was feeling scared and in need of the reassurance that *I* receive from the group. So there was projection on my part, and acting out of my feelings onto the group.

As it happened, these were the elements that were figural for Bruce. His mother was highly intrusive physically, emotionally, and sexually. As the object of unhealthy confluence in his childhood, much of Bruce's ongoing emotional work was to maintain a sense of boundaried separateness. My boundary confusion over who I was helping in my email (was I helping the group or myself?) triggered old feelings of confluence and intrusion. My liberal politics were no consolation to Bruce. "My parents were leftists, and they nearly destroyed us," he said pointedly. It took a willingness on both of our parts to unpack the feelings that were getting stirred up in order to repair the rupture to safety that had occurred for him. In this instance, making space for and taking the risk of finding out what Bruce was feeling was critical in initiating a dialogue that led to repair of a rupture that had occurred in the group.

The mix of feelings that I experienced in response to Bruce's work that day is worth looking at, I believe, because it helps illustrate resistances to and rewards of undertaking the shadow of the leader work. I was more than a little anxious about Bruce's distress because I did not know what was underneath it. On the other side of the coin, I was excited to hear about what Bruce was feeling. One of the rewards of doing the shadow of the leader work in GGT is that one never knows what direction things are going to take. It is a journey of inclusion into many distinct phenomenologies and narratives in the group. Each person has a frame of reference that is uniquely their own. I have found that being open to each point of view can be a mind- and heart-expanding journey for a GGT leader.

Martin Buber (1992, p. 40) describes a "narrow ridge" that is the meeting place between I and Thou. I appreciate Buber's imagery when doing this shadow of the leader work. It is a narrow ridge because there is no other presence in the entire universe quite like that of this particular leader, with her unique history, experience, body, and consciousness. At the same time, each group member is utterly unique in the details of her history, life experience, and awareness. We meet at a unique moment in our personal and collective histories. This meeting in this moment is like no other, and as such it is a source of amazement, wonder, dialogue, and repair of rupture, if we let it be so.

The Leader's Authority and the Group Member's Authority

It is necessary for the leader to exercise her authority throughout the life of the gestalt group. In order to attract members to the group initially, to lead the group through its various phases, to help members deal with their life problems, to inspire hope and to lead the group through difficulties, the leader tries to use her authority benevolently for the good of the group. The leader is the gatekeeper, the limit-setter with the final word, the one imbued with a special authority to confront members, to praise them, to shape the norms and culture of the group. How, then, to work with this authority in such a way that helps group members find their own power, yet does not undermine the leader's ability to lead? The answer lies in a *process orientation* that makes space for each member's perceptions, feelings, and fantasies toward the leader, about other members, and about the process itself. With a commitment to dialogue, the leader evokes from the group the shadow side of experience in the group including the membership's experience of leadership in the group. This helps keep life in the group real, helps the group from overly idealizing the leader, and helps the leader avoid addiction to being idealized or otherwise loved by the group.

Gestalt Groups Can Thrive When Leaders Continue to Do Their Own Growth Work

The GGT leader's commitment to personal and professional growth is essential to the vitality of the group. The leader who invests in personal therapy and ongoing clinical consultation, and stays involved with the professional community, is developing a support network that will benefit both herself and the groups she leads. It is this support that allows the leader to maintain a commitment to sometimes difficult and challenging dialogue around the shadow side of group life. It has been our experience that the membership can feel the leadership's willingness to access support and will respond positively to the leader who has cultivated strong support for her clinical work and her personal development. The membership's awareness of the leadership's support increases the confidence of group members in the capacity of the leader and other group members to hold them with all their feelings. This increased confidence lends a sense of safety and vitality, allowing the group to thrive.

Belonging in a Flawed Yet Loving Group

When group members are given support and permission to articulate the deeper undercurrents of group life, the group becomes a place where change happens not because the group leader is extraordinarily talented (although she may be), but because the group leader has fostered a culture where truth can be spoken, and where there is ongoing commitment to the dialogue (Yontef, 1988). The group becomes analogous to a family that, while far from perfect, has the ability to talk about what goes on in the family, and thereby builds deep bonds of attachment through intimate contact.

In the end, it is not the articulation of the shadow alone that changes lives. Articulating the undercurrents in group life is just a necessary step along the way to intimacy, love, and attachment. It is the unsentimental yet deeply accepting love that forms in the gestalt group that changes lives. When group members feel seen, shadow sides and all, when they can speak their truth about the group and its leaders and continue to be accepted, then they are on the road to achieving an authentic sense of belonging. There is nothing quite so healing as the feeling of being seen as a valuable and capable member of the group who is loved for who one is and is valued for sharing one's voice. Similarly, when the leaders of the group are seen with their strengths and talents, along with their flaws and shortcomings that can be talked about and worked through, the leaders can be felt in their humanness and can serve as role models for group members who wish to find their own humane power. The leader and fellow group members become a living part of each member's life, creating the ground for the emergence of stronger relationships, greater creativity, self-confidence, and self-acceptance.

Notes

1 An earlier version of this chapter first appeared as an article in *Gestalt Review* (2013, *17*(2), 178–189).
2 Please see Robert Stolorow's (1987) analogous concept of the repetitive and selfobject dimensions of psychoanalysis.
3 We have adopted the somewhat cumbersome terms *membership* and *leadership* as opposed to *members* and *leaders* in group work for a number of reasons. First, when we speak of the leadership, we could be speaking about one

or more people who are leading the group. Second, speaking of the membership and leadership allows us to point not just to an individual person but to
also think of that person fulfilling a role for the group that has both personal
and archetypal characteristics.
4 Yvonne Agazarian (2004) has made an important contribution to group therapy technique in emphasizing the importance of subgrouping. Instead of voicing support for a member coming forth, she invites other group members to
come and join the risk taker in the theory that it is safer to come forth as
part of a subgroup than to do so on one's own. In a similar vein, Gordon
Wheeler has discussed the importance of sharing in the reduction of shame in
men's groups. When one member comes forward with shameful feelings, he
guides the group in sharing their own shame rather than voicing support—as
he posits that giving support without taking the risk of sharing similar feelings
has the paradoxical effect of increasing shame. See also related discussions of
shame and scapegoating in the work of Ariedne Beck (1981) and Anne Alonso
(Alonso & Rutan, 1993).

References

Agazarian, Y. (2004). *Systems-centered therapy for groups*. London: Karnac
Books.
Aledort, S. L. (2009). Excitement: A crucial marker for group psychotherapy.
Group, *33*(1), 45–63.
Alonso, A., & Rutan, J. S. (1993). Character change in group therapy. *International
Journal of Group Psychotherapy*, *43*(4), 439–451.
Beck, A. P. (1981). Developmental characteristics of the system-forming process.
In J. E. Durkin (Ed.), *Living groups: Group psychotherapy and general system
theory*. New York: Brunner/Mazel.
Buber, M. (1992). *On intersubjectivity and cultural creativity*. Chicago,
IL: University of Chicago Press.
Cole, P. (1998). Affective process in psychotherapy: A gestalt therapist's view.
Gestalt Journal, *XXI*(1), 49–72.
Feder, B. (2006). *Gestalt group therapy: A practical guide*. New Orleans, LA:
Gestalt Institute Press.
Polster, E. (1995). *A population of selves: A therapeutic exploration of personal
diversity*. San Francisco, CA: Jossey-Bass.
Polster, E., & Polster, M. (1974). *Gestalt therapy integrated*. New York: Vintage.
Stolorow, R., Brandchaft, B., & Atwood, G. (1987). *Psychoanalytic treatment: An
intersubjective approach*. Hillsdale, NJ: Analytic Press.
Wheeler, G., & Jones, D. (2003). Finding our sons: A male–male gestalt. In R. Lee
& G. Wheeler (Eds), *The voice of shame: Silence and connection in psycho-
therapy* (pp. 61–100). Hillsdale, NJ: Analytic Press.
Yontef, G. (1988). *Awareness, dialogue and process*. Gouldsboro, ME: Gestalt
Journal Press.

Chapter 5

Creating and Sustaining a Relational Group Culture

This chapter is written in Daisy's voice

D. W. Winnicott (1971) taught us that the *self* of the baby is born in the gaze of the mother. This is true for the baby and no less true for us throughout our lives. It is only in relationship with an empathic other that we can understand ourselves and develop into our fullness. In the psychotherapy office, the empathic other is the therapist—ideally, a therapist who sees the client as they are and holds the vision of the client's fully developed self. In GGT, the group itself becomes the empathic other and the holding environment. Over time, members of a gestalt therapy group allow themselves to be truly seen by the group. This means allowing their "child self" to emerge—revealing old hurts, longings, fears and confusions. A mature group will be able to hold these aspects with both sensitivity and solidity, allowing the member to explore their vulnerabilities and begin to move toward increased integration and wholeness.

In order to develop a relational group culture, the first requirement is to gather a group of people capable of generating and sustaining such a culture. What does this mean in practical terms?

In my beginning years as a group therapist there was a widely espoused belief that member selection was not particularly important. Any gathering of willing people could be helped (by the wise group leader) to tap into their common humanity, develop empathy and compassion for one another, and build a group to support the members' development.

Today, many group therapists have traveled a far distance in the opposite direction. It is not an uncommon practice for group therapists to use a complex process of member selection that can include extensive questionnaires and multiple screening interviews. Every effort is made to find a good balance of genders, ages, educational levels, and so on (unless, of course, the group is specifically designed for a particular population such as a gay men's group or an older adults group). According to this screening approach, there should be no "outliers," for example a single man or a single person significantly older than the rest.

We have found something to recommend both approaches to group selection. We do strive to achieve a balance, and hope that group members will find others in the group with whom they can connect. For example, it can be difficult to be the only person of color in an otherwise all-white group, the only Jewish person in an otherwise non-Jewish group, the only gay person in an otherwise straight group, and so on. On the other hand, a perfect balance is often impossible to achieve, and with sufficient support and dialogue, imbalances in group composition can be worked with and can ultimately strengthen the group and all of its members. I think particularly of a group that included one man, Hari, a 65-year-old native of Nepal.

Hari's style of relating and his philosophy of life were in distinct contrast to those of the other group members. Hari struggled for a while to find his footing. Other members accused him of pontificating (often true!) and failing to relate to the struggles of others. It was in his relationship with Lisa, a young woman in her thirties, that Hari was finally able to connect in an emotionally honest, heartfelt way. Lisa talked frequently in the group about her mother who had abandoned her at a very young age. Not surprisingly, Lisa carried a great deal of grief and anger over the abandonment and the rest of the group was caring and supportive with her. Hari, however, had a different perspective. Having been raised in the Hindu tradition, he carried a strong belief in Karma and the idea of reincarnation. He grew impatient with Lisa, telling her more than once that she needed to practice acceptance and develop a wider view of life. Finally, Lisa "lost it." She burst into tears and angrily told Hari that he didn't understand her pain and that his philosophizing was anything but helpful.

Hari was taken aback. He was silent for the rest of the group meeting. When the group reconvened, however, he had clearly done some thinking about his stance. He was able to apologize to Lisa and they both agreed on the difficulty of bridging the gap in age and experience. The truth was, though, that Hari was developing very fatherly feelings for Lisa. It pained him for her to be angry at him. Recognizing this, Lisa started to let him in to provide some of the parenting she had so sorely lacked in her life. They continued to become irritated by and argumentative with each other, much as an actual father and daughter might. It was increasingly clear how significant they were to each other. When Hari announced that he was moving away and leaving the group, there were authentic tears from both him and Lisa. Both had moved past their quite distinct differences to offer each other a kind of intimacy and even love that surprised them both. This is just one example of the serendipity that so often occurs in a group which has a strong relational culture and can truly hold its members.

When interviewing a prospective group member we ask ourselves two questions: Is this someone who can entertain multiple perspectives (i.e., can the potential group member recognize that their way of understanding a given situation is not the only valid way)? Does this person appear to have a reasonably developed capacity for self-reflection? If the answer to either of these questions is "no," the interviewee is probably not a good prospect for GGT.

To be a bit more specific, we look for evidence of the following characteristics when choosing a new group member:

A capacity for empathy—Is the person interested in the emotional experience of others? Is he able to "feel with" the other even if his life experience has been quite different?

An ability to self-reflect—The ability to self-reflect refers to a person's understanding that they are inevitably a player in the drama; that it is impossible to be an "innocent bystander." When the inevitable misunderstandings and hurt feelings arise in a group, it is vitally important that each member has (or is able to develop) the realization that they are not just a "victim" but rather a contributor—unwittingly or otherwise—to the difficulty. When all participants—including the silent ones—can begin to understand and acknowledge their part in the interpersonal difficulties that arise in group, then resolution and increased connection become possible. If a group member is unable to move from a self-righteous stance to one of mutual understanding and forgiveness, then the group is seriously hampered in its development of a relational culture.

An ability to appreciate the validity of multiple narratives—It's an important tenet of GGT that "all the voices in the field need to be heard in order to understand the field" (Gordon Wheeler, personal communication, March 11, 2013). In a group, this means that each member (including the leader) has a unique perspective on what is happening in the group and, accordingly, no member (including the leader) is the possessor of "The Truth." It is only when all perspectives are respectfully taken into account that a meaningful understanding of the group can be brought about. The person unable to allow for the validity of multiple narratives, who insists that they alone have a stranglehold on the truth, will prove to be a significant handicap to the group's progress in developing self-awareness and understanding of the process. The "single-truth" position can also be significantly alienating to other group members—particularly members of minority groups—when they feel like their experience is being discounted or ignored.

In an established group where the relational culture has been developed, it is often possible to integrate a new member rather quickly. More mature members may be comfortable with helping the newcomer understand the culture of the group and learn to participate more empathically.

Not only is this a gift to the newcomer, but it can feel quite validating and empowering to the older members to help pass on the group culture to the newcomer.

Member selection, of course, is only the first step in the development of a relational group culture. From the very first group meeting the leader must be alert to opportunities to foster relationality and educate members about the importance of it and also what it looks like.

For each of us, there lives a tendency to seek the safety and apparent self-sufficiency of assuming an alienated/contact-avoidant position in life along with a countervailing tendency to risk the vulnerability and excitement of assuming a relational/contactful position. The more we can attune ourselves to our inner worlds, the more we become aware that we have both a longing for intimacy and a countervailing fear/anxiety about the painful possibilities that intimacy might open us up to. It is in relationship that we have been wounded and it is only in relationship that we can be healed.

Allowing ourselves to expose our vulnerabilities and be open to the possibilities of intimacy and connection requires a good bit of courage. It also requires an environment that is "safe enough." Will someone reach out a hand when we stumble? Will our risking be recognized and appreciated?

A successful group supports members in nurturing their relational/contactful strivings while, at the same time, coming to understand and work with their alienated/contact-avoidant tendencies. In the beginning phases of a group, most of this responsibility is, of necessity, carried by the leader. However, if the group is progressing well, the members become more and more capable of attuning to and holding each other. This allows the leader to step back from a highly active role and increasingly rely on "the wisdom of the group." As Laura Perls put it: the gestalt therapist should "do as much as necessary and as little as possible." (Bud Feder, personal communication, April 23, 2016). From my perspective as a group leader, there are few things more exciting and validating than the feeling that the group is sailing under its own steam. Although I certainly still fill a significant space in holding the group and its members, there is an increasing feeling of reciprocity—the group is also acting as a container for me.

For many of us, high anxiety can result in succumbing to the power of our alienated/contact-avoidant tendencies. The beginning of a new group is definitely a situation of high anxiety for almost everyone. As members enter the group room, their tendency is often to sit silently, not making eye contact, waiting for the leader to begin. Here, a simple social cue from the leader can be enormously helpful: "I'm glad to see everyone's arrived. Let's go around the circle and say our names and a couple of words about how we're feeling right now." An opening like this not only alleviates some of the initial anxiety but also gives group members a strong indication of how the group is to develop. Everyone's voice will be heard (all the voices of the field), our focus will be on our emotional life, and we will deal with our anxiety by starting to relate to each other (from a relational/contactful position) rather than by retreating into self-protective silence (an alienated/contact-avoidant position). Over time, the group develops a comfort with the relational culture and a deepening understanding of each other, and members become able to both support and confront each other in ways that enrich the group process.

Throughout the life of the group, the GGT leader seeks to support connectedness and intimacy among group members. Educating group members so as to create a group culture of relationality and connection continues throughout the life of the group. This education begins during the initial interview(s). In the initial interview, as the leader is considering whether a prospective member will make a good addition to the group, there is also an opportunity to talk with the potential group member about expectations. This educational process begins with the initial interviews and continues in some way until the member's last day in the group. In the beginning phases we teach how to join the group relationally. In the middle phases we teach how to work with each other and hang in with each other relationally. When a member leaves, we educate about ending and letting go relationally.

Whenever a group adds a new member, in some ways it can be considered to be a new group. Accordingly, it behooves the leader to revisit some of the basics. This "grounds" the new member while at the same time serving as a reminder to long-term members and provides an opportunity for them to bring up questions or, perhaps, old injuries previously unattended to.

I sometimes find it useful to introduce the "rules" of group in a rather humorous way by saying something like, "I often use this illustration with children, but I've found it's just as helpful for us adults!" The illustration goes like this: "There are five rules for group, just like the five fingers on your hand. First is the thumb; it points back at me." (Demonstrating.) "This rule says 'I speak for myself.' Next is the pointer; it points directly at you! It says 'I speak directly to the person I'm talking to; I don't talk *about* others.' Next is your middle finger—the strong one. It says 'I speak my truth.' Then comes your fourth finger; it's the most vulnerable one. It says 'I talk about my feelings and vulnerabilities.' The little finger says 'I'm the one who connects.'" (Demonstrate pinkies linking with other people's pinkies as any Girl Scout will remember!)

Going through this little demonstration usually gets a laugh, easing the tension. But it also makes a vivid imprint on group members that can be referred back to over time. Most importantly, this "children's" demonstration lays a foundation for a group culture of connectedness and relationality.

A relational group culture generates the atmosphere of a holding environment, analogous to the way in which a good enough family can hold the child. As in the good enough family, each member is appreciated for what they bring to the family, and compassion is demonstrated for each member's challenges, stuck places, actings out, and fixed relational gestalts. Sometimes the group will need to contain a group member who loses their way for one reason or another, and at other times the group will need to encourage the group member to act more assertively. There is love for each group member, an appreciation that no other person could hold the unique place in the group that that individual person holds.

Facilitating and sustaining a relational group culture is one of the most important roles of the GGT leader. The relational group culture is initially generated by the work of the leader, but as the group forms, the relational culture belongs to all of the group's members. A relational group culture becomes a holding environment for the group members, allowing them to express what needs to be expressed, to contain what needs to be contained, to attach to each other, and ultimately, when the time comes for group members to leave or the group to end, to let go contactfully.

References

Wheeler, G. (2013). *Beyond individualism: Toward a new understanding of self, relationships, and experience*. New York: Taylor & Francis.

Winnicott, D. W. (1971). *Playing and reality*. London: Tavistock.

Chapter 6

Integrating the Scapegoat Leader

This chapter is written in the voices of both Daisy and Peter

One of the most valuable things we have learned from our study of groups derives from the work of Ariadne Beck and the Chicago Group Development Research Team. Beck (1981a, 1981b) has identified leadership roles that tend to emerge in groups: the Emotional Leader, the Defiant Leader and the Scapegoat Leader.[1] Her work has helped us understand group dynamics and processes, especially when difficult and challenging interactions arise in the group. In this chapter, we discuss Beck's ideas about leadership roles and provide case examples demonstrating how these ideas have helped us in our group work. We will focus primarily on the Scapegoat Leader. We do so because understanding the role of the Scapegoat Leader can be so helpful to gestalt group therapy leadership, whereas not understanding this dynamic can lead to much unnecessary difficulty in GGT.

Beck's research has shown that group members will tend to arise within every group who will fulfill the roles of Emotional Leader, Defiant Leader, and Scapegoat Leader. Beck recommends identifying who these leaders are, and providing special consideration of each leader's needs, potential contributions, and the needs of the group in relation to these leaders in various phases of group development. As gestalt therapists, we are careful not to reify Beck's concepts, and do not see her analysis of the leadership roles as in any way replacing or diminishing the individuality of the group members we have identified as group leaders. Instead, we use Beck's ideas to help us understand certain patterns that can be difficult to navigate. Our caution about reifying Beck's leadership roles theory is similar to how we hold our understanding of character styles or attachment styles in individual gestalt therapy: we hold these ideas seriously yet lightly and in the background—using all categorical systems as a support to the work, being careful not to confuse the map with the territory. In Philip Lichtenberg's felicitous term, we hold Beck's theory about group leaders as "theoretical fiction" (personal communication, September 20,

1987)—holding her designations lightly, while using her model to help us navigate the sometimes stormy seas of GGT leadership.

We do not discuss our analysis of the leadership roles with our groups. Or to put it differently, we do not say who in the group we feel is holding the various roles. We would never say that we feel "Suzie is our Scapegoat Leader, Josh is our Defiant Leader, and Mary is our Emotional Leader." We find that this analysis is best kept confidential because it pertains primarily to the GGT leader's understanding and navigation of the group as a whole. Suzie is Suzie—she is not in any individual way a Scapegoat Leader, and making that designation of her would be objectifying of her. However, when approaching the group as a whole, understanding that Suzie is holding the Scapegoat Leader role will help the GGT leader protect both her and the group from scapegoating her. We will discuss the difference between identifying the Scapegoat Leader and the process of scapegoating later on in this chapter.

The Emotional and Defiant Leaders

The Emotional Leader is the group member who is most in tune with other group members. The Emotional Leader is able to empathize, confront, mirror, and generally be helpful to other group members. Obviously, the Emotional Leader plays an important role in keeping the group feeling cohesive and safe. We have found it important to support the Emotional Leader's contributions to the group and to support their feedback to other group members when it feels authentic to do so. Generally, the Emotional Leader has a very positive influence on the group culture, and that influence should be encouraged.

It is important for the GGT leader to let the Emotional Leader be the Emotional Leader. We have sometimes felt a pull as GGT leaders to compete with the Emotional Leader in an egoistic striving to be seen as wise and compassionate leaders. Such competitive impulses on the part of the GGT leader are best understood as "shadow of the leader" phenomena (see Chapter 4), and the truly wise GGT leader will contain such impulses to compete with the Emotional Leader. We have found it best to give the Emotional Leader plenty of space to influence the group and its members. There is a potency to the emotional supplies group members can give to each other. This potency can feel watered down when supplied by the GGT leader. Group members often feel, for example, that positive feedback is more authentic coming from other group members—after all, fellow group members aren't being paid to say something nice. Also, a well-placed confrontation can be very effective coming from a fellow group member. The Emotional Leader will often be the source of these gems that pass between group members. So, once you have identified your Emotional Leader, giving that person plenty of space to influence the group can be very effective.

The Defiant Leader is the group member who is most skeptical of the official GGT leader(s). The Defiant Leader often feels that there is something lacking in the GGT leader's method, skills, or approach. The Defiant Leader maintains a sense of distance from and even opposition to the GGT leader. One of the positive functions that the Defiant Leader plays for the group is to protect the group from overly idealizing the GGT leader. The Defiant Leader plays a democratizing function for the group, standing as a bulwark against blind allegiance to the GGT leader. The Defiant Leader can be thought of as the "loyal opposition." As a GGT leader, it can be helpful to keep in mind that the Defiant Leader fulfills this healthy function for the group: reminding the group that we meet as equals even though the GGT leader has a different set of boundaries and responsibilities than other group members. It is therefore important that the GGT leader be respectful of the Defiant Leader and be aware of staying open when the Defiant Leader criticizes them overtly or covertly. When the GGT group can see that the Defiant Leader is respected by the GGT leader, a sense of safety begins to form in the knowledge that the group can function democratically, without a need to mirror or idealize the GGT leader. We have found it helpful to give the Defiant Leader an abundance of respect and plenty of leeway to express dissatisfaction with the current group leadership.

Understanding the role of the Defiant Leader helps the GGT leader maintain balance and composure when the GGT leader's competence and clinical choices are being questioned by the Defiant Leader. With an understanding that, in a healthy group, a group member will likely arise to oppose them, and provide the group members with an alternative to idealizing them, this kind of opposition can be felt by the GGT leader as normal and healthy. Rather than becoming defensive, the GGT leader makes plenty of space for the Defiant Leader's opposition, thereby promoting an egalitarian group culture that honors the perspective of all group members.

The Scapegoat Leader

The Scapegoat Leader presents many challenges and opportunities for the GGT leader. The Scapegoat Leader tends to be the group member who has most trouble fitting in, who perhaps says the wrong thing at the wrong time, and in general is the person that other group members would most likely "vote off the island." If you, as a group leader (or group member), think about the group member who evokes the strongest negative feelings for the greatest number of group members, then you will have, in all likelihood, identified your Scapegoat Leader.

The Scapegoat Leader frequently has difficulty staying in good quality contact with other group members and may be seen as the "lowest functioning" person in the group, yet they play an important leadership role in the group. The Scapegoat Leader might become more emotionally reactive or volatile than other group members, and may challenge the GGT leader or other group members in ways that raise the temperature of the group and the anxiety level of the group members. According to Beck (1981a, p. 53), the Scapegoat Leader typically "models the conflict between assertion of the self and conformity to the group." Because the Scapegoat Leader does not conform and is out of step, they challenge the group to be inclusive. The group must stretch itself emotionally; it must be compassionate and inclusive to integrate the Scapegoat Leader. The Scapegoat Leader's nonconformity is different from the Defiant Leader's challenge to the GGT leader. While the Defiant Leader poses a challenge to the direction in which the GGT leader is taking the group, and typically competes with the GGT leader, the Scapegoat Leader typically does not fit in with the group and is out of step with the GGT leader and/or the group.

Let us define *scapegoating* as unhealthy and unaware acting out of negative feelings that coalesce around the *Scapegoat Leader* (this is our definition, not Beck's). In this definition "scapegoating" is a verb. The people who are doing the scapegoating are the group members, and sometimes the group leaders. The job of the GGT leader is to refocus the group dialogue such that feelings group members hold toward the Scapegoat Leader are brought to awareness. In so doing, group members can take responsibility for how they respond to the Scapegoat Leader, which in turn helps set the stage for greater responsibility-taking by the Scapegoat Leader. When the group is engaged in scapegoating, the negative feelings that coalesce around the Scapegoat Leader feel as though they are *about* the Scapegoat Leader. However, when given enough support, feelings that appeared to be about the Scapegoat Leader turn out to be only *triggered* by the Scapegoat Leader, and live in one form or another in all group members.

We think that many experienced GGT leaders will recognize the experience of facilitating a gestalt group with a member who pushes the limits and boundaries of the group in some way. It is frequently tempting (and sometimes true) to categorize this individual as "disturbed" or "borderline personality disordered" or to put them in some other diagnostic category. While these diagnostic impressions may well be correct (Greenberg, 2016), as a *group* leader, the most important understanding is not of the *individual's* pathology. Instead, the most important perspective is to think about the role this person is playing out for the group-as-a-whole. When the GGT leader appreciates that, from the group-as-a-whole perspective, this person may be playing out the Scapegoat Leader role, she can then hold the group-as-a-whole issues in the foreground rather than the individual-level issues of that person. Group-as-a-whole issues concern how the Scapegoat Leader is relating to the other group members. How is the group getting along with this member, and how is the member getting along with the group? These are much more salient issues than doing gestalt work at the individual level with the Scapegoat Leader in the group.

As we will see in the examples below, working prematurely with the Scapegoat Leader at the individual or intrapsychic level may have the unintended consequence of separating the Scapegoat Leader from the rest of the group, pathologizing them in the eyes of the other group members, and in fact may lead to the scapegoating of that person. In our view, the GGT leader must do much work toward integrating the Scapegoat Leader with the rest of the group before effective individual-level work with the Scapegoat Leader can be effectively undertaken in the group.

We have found that vital grounding for meaningful individual-level work with the Scapegoat Leader (and arguably for all group members) is the experience of being held by the group as a valued and respected member of the group. When the GGT leader puts her energy into supporting the Scapegoat Leader's connection with other group members and into helping the group make emotional and compassionate space for the Scapegoat Leader, then the ground is prepared for individual-level work with the Scapegoat Leader later in the life of the group. When the necessary work of supporting the Scapegoat Leader's integration into the group has not been adequately attended to, individual-level work can become frustrating and alienating for the Scapegoat Leader and can create a sense in other group members that the Scapegoat Leader does not really belong in the group.

Integrating the Scapegoat Leader is a delicate business, and can take even experienced GGT leaders by surprise. Let me (Peter) recount a mistake I made recently with a group member who clearly was the group's Scapegoat Leader:

> Doris was a disabled Asian American woman in GGT. She had missed a large number of groups, had a history of conflict with other group members, and had a tendency to dominate and take a lot of group time. Because Doris was a disabled person of color from a working-class background, I had taken a particular interest in her professional development and was quite invested in mentoring her in forging her personal and professional life-path. So ... when she held forth in group, taking an unusual amount of time with recounting challenges in her career and personal life, I was in a very mirroring mode with her, listening intently, and giving a lot of verbal and non-verbal support. In my focus on mirroring and supporting at the individual level, I failed to be aware of the fact that other group members

were getting frustrated and bored with Doris's dominance of group time. I even failed to be fully aware of the fact that several members got up to use the bathroom while she was speaking. When she was done, I gave her positive feedback, but several group members became angry with her for dominating group time and strongly criticized her. Doris was shocked by the group's feedback. While I tried to bring the group's anger to me and to take responsibility for the rupture that had occurred in the group, it was too little, too late. Doris abruptly quit the group after this session. I was shaken and deeply disappointed by these developments.

I must say that it took me some time to fully understand the nature of my mistakes. But here is my analysis of where I went wrong. First, although in retrospect it is clear that Doris was playing the role of Scapegoat Leader with this group, I failed to grasp that at the time. If I had understood that Doris was in the role of Scapegoat Leader and that from a group-as-a-whole perspective it would have been profitable to put issues of her connectedness to the group in the foreground rather than on mirroring her, I could have avoided many problems that ensued for both Doris and for the group. What I would do differently now is to say to her after a few minutes of monopolizing group time: "I can see that you have many challenges you are dealing with! I am also aware that other group members may have feelings that they want to share—so how would it be to hear from others?"

Another piece that I missed is the *shadow of the leader* material. The shadow of the leader material is that which is out of awareness of the leader within the field conditions of the group. The group is impacted by this shadow of the leader material, whereas this material is often outside of the leader's awareness. In the situation with Doris, the shadow of the leader aspect was my guilt around my privilege and my whiteness. Out of my awareness, I was acting this out with Doris. I had given her a partial scholarship on the group fee, and had taken a particular interest in her development. Consciously, this felt to me like a good deed, and consistent with my values as a gestalt therapist. In the shadows, however, and felt by the group members, but not yet by me, was the other side of the coin: that I was giving Doris special consideration, and that I was more attentive to her personal development than to her relationships with other group members.[2]

Defusing Scapegoating with Contact and Dialogue

When we feel that scapegoating is occurring, we try to pull back the zoom lens and think about the Scapegoat Leader's relationship with the group. As gestalt therapists, our primary mode of interaction is contact and dialogue, not interpretation, so we are not in the business of offering the group a psychoanalytic interpretation of who or what the Scapegoat Leader represents for the rest of the group. Instead, we are engaged in an interactive group process, guided by the principles and aesthetics of dialogue, to bring awareness and better quality contact to the relationship between the Scapegoat Leader and the group.

Dialogue consists of inclusion, presence, and commitment to the dialogue. When engaged in a process of moving away from the scapegoating, we emphasize *commitment to the dialogue* and *presence* in order to achieve *inclusion*. The GGT leader turns her attention to the dialogue between the Scapegoat Leader and the group. (Please note that it is often important to *not* focus on dialogue between the GGT leader and the Scapegoat Leader when in the initial stages of undoing the scapegoating for the reasons discussed in the paragraphs above. That work will come later, when the Scapegoat Leader is more fully integrated into the group.) In working on the dialogue between the Scapegoat Leader and the group, Yontef's (1988) elements of dialogue are a useful guide to group facilitation, as described in the following sections.

Commitment to the Dialogue (Objects of Contemplation for the Group Leader)

- Am I aiming at a *fix* of the Scapegoat Leader rather than being committed to the process of *being with* the Scapegoat Leader and the group?
- Can I tolerate the discomfort of being present with conflict between the Scapegoat Leader and other group members?

Commitment to the Dialogue (Examples of Interventions)

- The GGT leader points out the friction she is observing between the group and the Scapegoat Leader, and points out what may be gained by working those issues through.
- The GGT leader expresses directly or indirectly her interest in better understanding what is happening between the group and the Scapegoat Leader.
- When the Scapegoat Leader says or does something that upsets other group members, the GGT leader must gently remind the group that "all the voices of the field" are vital to our understanding and growth as a group.

Presence (Objects of Contemplation for the Group Leader)

- How do I feel about the Scapegoat Leader's difficulties with the rest of the group?
- Do these difficulties bring up feelings of incompetence or impotence in me?
- Do such feelings make me want to "fix" the Scapegoat Leader?
- How can I lend my authentic authority to building safety for the Scapegoat Leader and for the group?
- How can I lend my presence to building bridges between the Scapegoat Leader and the rest of the group?

Presence (Examples of Interventions)

- The GGT leader lends specific support or protection to the Scapegoat Leader if he feels that the group is excluding or ganging up on him.
- The GGT leader redirects the group if a number of people are "piling on" criticism of the Scapegoat Leader.
- The GGT leader comments on the group "dropping" the Scapegoat Leader.[3]
- The GGT leader works with the Scapegoat Leader in a dyad to help him share his feelings in ways that are more inviting to the person with whom he is communicating.

Inclusion (Objects of Contemplation for the Group Leader)

- How might it feel to be in the shoes of the Scapegoat Leader within the social context of the group?
- How might it feel to other group members to be in group with the Scapegoat Leader?
- How does the Scapegoat Leader feel with regard to being included in/excluded from the group?

Inclusion (Examples of Interventions to Promote Inclusion)

- The GGT leader actively listens to the Scapegoat Leader and shares with him what she has heard.
- The GGT leader facilitates dyadic contact between the Scapegoat Leader and another group member focused on empathy and compassion.
- The GGT leader shares with the Scapegoat Leader how she imagines the Scapegoat Leader may be feeling and checks that out with them.

We have sometimes seen GGT leaders become inadvertently involved in a scapegoating process by getting stuck at the individual level of intervention with the Scapegoat Leader. When the facilitator gets involved in a confrontation with the Scapegoat Leader that appears to be important and potentially valuable, the GGT leader can unfortunately end up further alienating the Scapegoat Leader from the group. If the GGT leader gets caught up in a frustrating piece of individual work such as trying to help the Scapegoat Leader take responsibility for her actions or look at her blind spots, or trying to foster contact and awareness with the Scapegoat Leader by working through the issues at the individual level, this can often be unhelpful. What the GGT leader here may be missing is that the issues are better approached from the group-as-a-whole level. Before individual-level work can proceed, the Scapegoat Leader must be integrated into the group. The GGT leader's job then is to think about the Scapegoat Leader from a field perspective. How can they be helped to receive more support from the group and to be better integrated into the group? How can the group be helped to create more space for the Scapegoat Leader?

Vignette 1: Helping the Scapegoat Leader Move Out of the Therapist Role

Fred is a senior therapist with a long career in the mental health field. He entered a weekly therapy group with "an attitude." He tended to assume the role of group leader rather than that of group member, giving unwanted advice to other group members and showing little of his own vulnerability. Fred considered himself a "veteran" of therapy groups and had little patience for other group members' input or feedback. He was focused on us, the group leaders, with a combination of the need for a lot of attention and a competitive edge. He was very irritating to other group members in that he seemed disinterested in and condescending to them. He was irritating to us in that he was both attention seeking and very competitive. It is no surprise that Fred was quickly becoming the focal point of group anger. We could see that a scapegoating process was beginning to get enacted with the group, ourselves, and Fred.

In order to move away from scapegoating, we focused the group process on dialogue around Fred's relationships with other group members and on group members' relationships with him. Our purpose was to explore the quality of those relationships as they were unfolding in the group. Our thinking was that, if the group could talk about what was happening with Fred, there would be less need to act out a scapegoating process.

We simply posed the question: "How are people doing with Fred?" This brought up a discussion of people feeling hurt by and angry with his attitude toward them. It also brought up group members' positive feelings toward Fred. Although this discussion was initially uncomfortable for all concerned, it was also settling for members because we were talking about what was actually happening in the group. Fred was defensive at times, accusatory at times, but also interested in what he was learning about himself. We gave Fred a lot of support by highlighting the positive things that were being said, making sure that he took the time to take those things in but was also hearing the difficult things that were being shared by group members. Also, we gave support to group members who were saying difficult things, appreciating how they were communicating respectfully and not putting Fred down.

Over time, both Fred and the group were able to talk about the difficulties he was having with group members and with the leaders. Being able to talk about the difficulties in relating with Fred defused the scapegoating and let Fred begin to feel the support of the other group members. With a new sense of *belonging* achieved, Fred and the group were safe from scapegoating and the stage was now set for more individual-level work, focusing on Fred's family of origin story, his trauma history, his substance abuse issues, and his relationships. As the group came to know Fred's story, the sense of connection with him increased. Not surprisingly, his behaviors involving being dismissive of other group members, of being demanding and competitive with the group leaders, and of inappropriately taking on the role of therapist in the group almost completely disappeared. Group members came to deeply appreciate Fred, and he came to feel much better about himself.

Notes

1 Beck also identifies the Task Leader, who typically is the official group leader. The Task Leader attends to all of the logistical aspects of group leadership such as setting the time, fee, place, and so on.

2 Another issue here is the fee reduction I (Peter) had offered Doris. I did not make this fee reduction known to other group members, as I consider this a confidence to be held in the boundary of the leader and member. In my view, the privilege of disclosure of the fee reduction lies with the group member and not with the group leader. In our groups, a group member is free to disclose a scholarship we have given, but we do not make such disclosures. Other group leaders have put forth the policy that all financial matters should be known by all group members—that there be full financial transparency. Although things did not turn out well with Doris's group involvement, we have offered fee reductions to many group members over the years for a variety of reasons. These fee reductions have rarely been disclosed by the group members, and in the great majority of cases, we have seen no harm come of holding this confidence.

3 We use the term "drop" to denote a pattern wherein a group member makes a comment or shares something, and others in the group do not pick up on it. For example, if Suzy says to the group that this is the anniversary of her father's death and no one picks up on it, the leader might ask Suzy, "Did you feel dropped after you shared about this being the anniversary of your father's death?"

References

Beck, A. P. (1981a). A study of group phase development and emergent leadership. *Group*, 5(4), 48–54.

Beck, A. P. (1981b). Developmental characteristics of the system-forming process. In J. E. Durkin (Ed.), *Living groups: Group psychotherapy and general system theory*. New York: Brunner/Mazel.

Greenberg, E. (2016). *Borderline, narcissistic, and schizoid adaptations: The pursuit of love, admiration, and safety*. New York: Greenbrooke Press.

Wallin, D. (2007). *Attachment in psychotherapy*. New York: Guilford Press.

Yontef, G. (1988). *Awareness, dialogue and process*. Gouldsboro, ME: Gestalt Journal Press.

Chapter 7

Working with the Group as a Whole

This chapter is written in Daisy's voice

Vignette 1: When the Road to Hell is Paved with Good Intentions

I was attending an intensive four-day gestalt training workshop with Joshua, a well-known gestalt therapist, and the group had been going well. However, on the third day, Mary, a group member, became visibly upset with Joshua. Until the third day, Mary would have called her group experience a success, but something had happened between her and Joshua in the morning that felt quite wounding to Mary. Though Mary had never met Joshua before, she had read his writings. She idealized him and felt she had a tremendous amount to learn from him. A major reason for her coming from a distant city to the workshop was her hope of connecting with Joshua. In the morning group session, she had worked up her nerve, and asked Joshua some questions about his books. He responded curtly that the process group was not the place to discuss theoretical issues. Mary felt his response to be dismissive, condescending, and shaming. She felt quietly devastated by the end of the morning.

This feeling was still very present with Mary after the lunch break. She returned for the afternoon session with very strong feelings of hurt and anger toward Joshua, which she expressed at first with great difficulty and with mounting anger as her feelings gathered momentum. The group watched as Mary became more and more visibly distressed. I watched as Joshua struggled with listening to, containing, and coping with Mary's emotionality in the group. She seemed to unravel and become increasingly unreachable. The more emotional and "unreasonable" Mary became, the more a distinct polarity developed between her and the rest of the group. As she got more upset, the rest of the group, including myself, became increasingly calm, distant, and "put together." We shifted into "helpful" mode. All attention was now focused on helping Mary. Mary clearly now felt to me like an outlier in the group; she appeared to be more emotional and less functional than other group members.

Joshua tried valiantly to maintain an empathic connection with Mary. He took responsibility for having been dismissive in the morning, and attempted in many ways to repair the rupture his earlier behavior had set in motion. He attempted to support Mary in looking at what may have been triggered for her. All was in vain. She was having none of his attempts at repair. I could see Joshua become increasingly exasperated. Mary escalated and threatened to walk out of the group. As I watched Joshua struggle to contain and reach Mary, I could practically hear his thoughts: "Why am I cursed with this acting out borderline personality in my group?" and "I've got to contain her or she is going to do damage to the whole group." If Joshua had been thinking this way, it certainly would have been understandable, but such thinking may have caused Joshua to focus on an aspect of the situation which led the group to a dead end— Mary's individual psychology and history. The more he sought to work with Mary around her anger, her history of anger, and her history of feeling dismissed in her family of origin, the more distressed she became, the angrier she became with him, and the more alienated she became from the rest of the group. As she dominated and repeatedly threatened to leave the workshop during the afternoon session, other group members, including myself, became anxiously detached from and annoyed with Mary.

I found myself thinking thoughts about Mary such as "I don't have problems like this" and "Let me see if I can find a way to offer Mary some helpful advice." As I looked around the group, it was clear that other members were also feeling emotionally removed. One after another, we made efforts to reach out and "fix" Mary. In the blink of an eye, the process of scapegoating Mary had begun. Since this was a therapist training group, the labeling of Mary as a "borderline personality" by group members and the leader was almost palpable, although of course unsaid. Joshua's good intentions had led both him and the group into a dead end—that of scapegoating a group member. Let us explore the nature of the scapegoating and look at some alternative approaches that a GGT leader might have taken with Mary and the group.

First, let's look at an alternative way to think about the kind of challenges that a group member such as Mary poses for the group and the leader. While it is possible that Mary really is too unstable to function in the group, it is far more likely that her difficulty with functioning in the group is due to a combination of factors, including the question of how well connected she is feeling with the rest of the group. In her excellent chapter on intensive gestalt workshops in *Beyond the Hot Seat Revisited*, Ruth Ronall (2008, p. 220) states, "I put the main stress on the group-as-a-whole, making room for the individual, and not so much on the individual making a place for him/herself." Here, Ronall is emphasizing the importance of each member feeling connected with others in the group, and the responsibility the leader must take in facilitating the group in finding its way to reach out to each member in a way that feels good and connected. Ronall's comments are especially apt in dealing with the challenges of scapegoating. As we will see with various pathways up from scapegoating, they all involve the group leader's attention to the group's connections to its most vulnerable individual member: the Scapegoat Leader.

So let's explore several alternative pathways that Joshua might have tried that put the emphasis on the whole group while making room for Mary.

Alternative Group Leadership Pathway 1: Protecting and Bringing Forth the Positive Contributions of the Scapegoat Leader

In a number of ways, both Mary and the group are colluding to scapegoat Mary in this group. Mary is colluding in her scapegoating by being demanding, blaming, and inconsolable. The group is colluding in scapegoating Mary by letting Mary carry all of the vulnerability and emotion in the group; by feeling defended in response to her and feeling superior to her. As we discussed in Chapter 6, it is important to understand that there is a difference between identifying the group's *Scapegoat Leader* (according to Ariadne Beck's (1981a) terminology) and the process of *scapegoating* that person. The main reason that we put energy into identifying the group's Scapegoat Leader is so that we can *prevent* that person from becoming scapegoated in the group. We do this by recognizing the Scapegoat Leader's positive contributions to the group and protecting that person in the group process. Now that we have established the difference between identifying the person who is fulfilling the role of the Scapegoat Leader for the group (a role that Beck says is inevitably played out in every group and carries with it many positive attributes) and the process of scapegoating that person (a process that is destructive both to the individual who is scapegoated and to the group), let's look at some of the characteristics of the Scapegoat Leader that Ariadne Beck (1981b, p. 14) describes:

> *[The Scapegoat Leader] is generally one step behind the group in understanding nonverbal messages, often asking for these messages to be made more explicit..*
>
> *In early phases of group [the Scapegoat Leader] may be the object of negative or hostile feelings in the context of discussions of normative issues and leadership selection. (In contrast to the Emotional Leader who is self-aware and assertive, the Scapegoat Leader appears to be assertive but not self-aware.)*

Both of these characteristics were very true of Mary in the group. She was out of sync with the rest of the group in terms of how much anger and intense emotion she was directing at the leader, and (partly because the group was in an early phase of its development) she was particularly vulnerable to becoming the object of negative and hostile feelings from the leader and other group members. Before we look at what the leader might do in this circumstance to protect Mary from getting scapegoated by the group, let us look at some of the positive characteristics that Beck (1981b, pp. 15–16) ascribes to the Scapegoat Leader:

> *In contrast to the way group perceives the Scapegoat Leader, he is actually open, willing to be self-disclosing, and willing to engage in ... give and take.*
>
> *[The Scapegoat Leader] [m]onitors and tests the boundary between what members are willing to say explicitly and what members wish to communicate implicitly, nonverbally or symbolically.*
>
> *[The] group uses [the] Scapegoat Leader to define certain identity boundaries of the group as a system; [the] Scapegoat Leader monitors inclusiveness issues.*

With Beck's observations about the Scapegoat Leader in mind, we can now think about another avenue Joshua may have used to navigate the difficulties with Mary in the group. These can be broadly understood as strategies to *protect and bring forth the positive contributions of the Scapegoat Leader*. It is vital that the GGT leader does all she can to protect the Scapegoat Leader from being ostracized and becoming the object of negative projections from the group. This is a tricky and sometimes counter-intuitive skill to develop. Just when the Scapegoat Leader is out of sync with the rest of the group, demanding the attention of the group, and frequently attacking the leader or another group member, the GGT leader needs to both attend sufficiently to the immediate issues the Scapegoat Leader is raising and help the group de-focus on the Scapegoat Leader. The best way to do this is to highlight the positive contributions that the Scapegoat Leader is bringing to the group, and to help other group members join with and appreciate the Scapegoat Leader.

Let's look at some of the ways in which Joshua could have included this perspective with Mary:

MARY: Joshua, the way you treated me this morning just devastated me. I came all this way to work with you and discuss your work, and you literally shut me down. I was so shocked when you said that the group was not the place to discuss your writings.

JOSHUA: I can see on your face how hurt you are. Is there more you want to tell me?

MARY: I have never been so humiliated in my life.

JOSHUA: I hear I really wounded you. Hurting you is the last thing I would want to do!

MARY: Well, thank you, but you didn't just hurt me, you have deeply wounded me, and I am thinking of leaving the workshop and going home.

JOSHUA: I'm so sorry that I've wounded you. Your leaving would be a huge loss for me and for the group. One thing I want to point out is that you are speaking up for yourself, which I certainly respect, and you are doing a real service for the group! No one else has done this so far, and it is so important that the group feel free to express negative feelings toward the leader! So I'm wondering if other people in the group are having negative feelings toward me, and haven't felt enough support to express them. I would be very interested in hearing about those!

At this point, other group members join in the group process, supporting Mary's leadership in opening up discussion around negative feelings toward the leader, and the expression of strong feelings and self-disclosure. Mary's role in the group is seen now as one of leadership rather than as an outlier and an object of projection from other group members.

Alternative Group Leadership Pathway 2: The Shadow of the Leader

The shadow of the leader work we discussed in Chapter 4 informs Joshua that when a group member such as Mary brings up something difficult that has occurred between her and him as the leader, she is presenting the group with an opportunity to open up vital dialogue around the group's experience of the leader. Mary is providing the group with an opportunity to deepen its connection with the leader by talking about some of the aspects of their experience of the leader that have remained out of awareness. Taken in this context, Mary's bringing forward of these issues with Joshua is an expression of her courage, rather than an expression of anything negative about her.

When Mary expresses her anger at Joshua for being dismissive of her in the morning session, Joshua can use the following principles to guide his contact with her.

Inclusion and Confirmation: Being Sure to Hear and Feed Back What Mary is Feeling and Thinking

MARY: Joshua, the way you treated me this morning just devastated me. I came all this way to work with you and discuss your work, and you literally shut me down. I was so shocked when you said that the group was not the place to discuss your writings.

JOSHUA: Oh my gosh, Mary, thank you so much for letting me know about how this impacted you. Please tell me more.

MARY: Well, it's ironic, isn't it, because much of your work is about shame, and then you went right ahead and shamed the hell out of me this morning! I could hardly believe it! I just feel like burying my head in the sand!

JOSHUA: The last thing I would want to do is to shame you, Mary. I can see that I have done that, and I am so sorry.

Presence: Sharing with Mary where Joshua Is and His Part In It

JOSHUA: You know, it is no accident that I have written about shame. You are finding out the hard way that I am prone to both feeling shame and shaming others. With all the work I have done on myself over the years in my own therapy, I find that I keep walking blindly into situations where I shame others out of my awareness. It always takes me by surprise! I can see now how my stuff spilled out onto you and I thank you for bringing it to my attention.

MARY: Yes, it really did spill onto me!

JOSHUA: Perhaps we can take some time together later this week to discuss your thoughts about my book?

MARY: Thank you, that would be great. And I appreciate your taking responsibility for what happened between us.

Commitment to the Ongoing Group Dialogue

JOSHUA [TO THE GROUP]: I imagine that Mary is not the only one in this group who has had a large or small shaming experience with me. I've been around long enough to know that I have a tendency to generate these experiences as a group leader. Since Mary has courageously blazed this trail, I'd really like to hear from other group members whom I may have hurt in this way. Letting me know is a great favor to me, because you are giving me an opportunity to repair hurts that I've caused that I'm probably unaware of.

Several group members come forward and process some past experiences with Joshua.

Discussion of Both Alternative Pathways

Both of these alternative pathways to working with Mary can be effective given the particular leader's personality and style and, of course, Mary's response.

These pathways have some things in common:

1. The leader is willing to hear Mary out and to validate her feelings.
2. The leader is willing to acknowledge his own piece of the problem.
3. The leader does not interpret Mary or suggest that the leader's offending behavior existed only in Mary's imagination.
4. The leader moves as quickly as he can to bring in the rest of the group.
5. Bringing in the rest of the group may be to support Mary or it may be to recognize what Mary is offering the group—to talk about her courage and service to the group in bringing up what has been unspoken. It might be to talk about the safety the members feel (or don't feel) in expressing anger or other "negative" feelings with the leader.
6. The leader works to normalize Mary's feelings. She isn't the only one who feels this way.
7. The leader moves to help the group express their own unexpressed feelings toward him.

In taking one of these alternative pathways, Joshua is not just dealing with the dyadic, two-person system of himself and Mary. Instead, he is bringing in the whole group. He is looking at the group-as-a-whole. This is a very different vantage point from which to perceive the group than the individual perspective. From the individual perspective in gestalt groups the leader might be working with any number of issues involving a group member's awareness, fixed gestalts or change process. On the other hand, when the group-as-a-whole is in the leader's foreground of awareness, the leader is focused on the well-being of the group. From the group-as-a-whole perspective, the work of the group is to find its way into making emotional space for each member of the group, helping each member feel respected and valued.

Shifting the Foreground Focus

One of the most important skills of the GGT leader is to develop the capacity to shift the lens through which she is viewing the issues in the group—to shift the background/foreground focus, putting the individual-level work into the background so that the group-as-a-whole issues can come to the foreground, and to shift again back to individual-level work. We have found that the strengths the *individual-level* work tends to give the group are a sense of context, depth, history, and empathy while *group-as-a-whole* issues tend to lend energy and cohesiveness (Yalom & Leszcz, 2005) and add to the esprit de corps.

As we discussed in Chapter 2, we consider there to be three basic levels of focus for the GGT leader: the individual, the dyadic and the group-as-a-whole. As a group leader, being able to shift the foreground focus from the individual level to the group-as-a-whole or dyadic level is a very important skill for gestalt group therapists to develop. We have found that the choices we make in this regard can have a profound impact on our groups. In this discussion, we will deal with when to shift the focus from the individual level to the group-as-a-whole level, leaving out for now issues of the dyadic level.

The first and most important rule of thumb we follow is to always keep the group-as-a-whole at least in the back of our minds when we are leading. We try to never forget that perspective. In other words, when we are leading groups, we are continually coming back to very basic questions about how things feel in the room. What are group members' communicating with their body language? Are they engaged? Bored? Are some people dominating and others checking out? Are one or more members late or out? The group-as-a-whole should not be a mysterious or highly theoretical way of perceiving the group. Instead, it is a down-to-earth sense of what is happening in the room. Making observations about the group-as-a-whole level and inviting the group to make their own observations helps group members build skills in observing and commenting on the group-as-a-whole level.

Vignette 2: Example of a Very Simple Group-as-a-Whole Commentary by the Leader

Group-as-a-whole observations need not be fancy, heady, or a big deal. For example, in one of our groups last week two members, Mara and Mark, announced that they were leaving group. This is their penultimate session. Mark, while having announced that he is leaving, is opening up new facets of ongoing issues that feel juicy. Daisy is leading the group.

DAISY: The group really seems to be energetic today. I'm noticing that people in the group are responding very energetically to Mark. Are other people noticing the energy?

ROSARIO: Well, I don't feel the group is energetic so much as we are feeling a little surprised that Mark is leaving with all of this stuff coming up.

MARK: I feel like the group is really paying attention to me and I appreciate that a lot.

MARA: I think that since Mark and I have decided to leave, the group has perked up energy-wise. I wonder if you guys are trying to make us stay!

AMY: You bet we are! Seriously, I think we are all feeling a little sad that you are leaving, and maybe we are trying to get you to stay so we don't have to miss you when you go!

You can see in the above example that Daisy invites a group-as-a-whole focus with a down-to-earth observation about the group, and group members make further observations about the group-as-a-whole naturally and organically. These conversations lend a sense of camaraderie and shared responsibility for understanding and speaking to the group process.

The basic task of the group is to promote the development of each individual group member. When the group is not in crisis, and there are no major conflicts brewing, then our basic mode of operating is to attend to the work of each individual group member, and let this unfold sometimes with intensive one-on-one contact between the leader and an individual group member and sometimes in the contact that occurs between group members facilitated by us, with the group leaders intervening as needed to keep the work moving forward and the group safe. So, as a rule of thumb, we can say that *when there is smooth sailing in the group, we will tend to put the emphasis on individual-level issues.*

Since GGT is comprised of human beings, conditions of smooth sailing usually do not prevail for long. When the waters get choppy due to issues such as conflicts between group members, scapegoating, conflicts with the leader, poor attendance, or boundary problems such as breaches of confidentiality, then we will tend to shift the focus away from the individual level and move to the group-as-a-whole level. Doing so helps to increase the group's capacity to stay in contact with one another through conflict while keeping the safety level manageable and tolerable. As a rule of thumb we can say that, *when the waters get choppy, we attend to the group-as-a-whole perspective.*

Vignette 3: Working through a Conflict with the Help of the Group

Kenneth had a tendency to speak faster and louder than other group members. He was an engineer and manager for a tech company. He was very unhappily married. While it took other members longer to express themselves, Kenneth would put his perspective out there fast and force-fully. During one group session, Michelle was talking about a difficulty in her marriage and Kenneth jumped in:

MICHELLE: I am really getting sick and tired of my husband's dependence on me. He wants to be with me all the time and I can't take it. He wants to have sex all the time, and I am just tired. I'm working and taking care of our kids. I have zero attraction to him!

KENNETH: Wow, Michelle, I would think you would be glad to have a husband who is into you! I think you take him for granted!

MICHELLE: Kenneth, why do you always feel you have the right to comment on my life? I don't get you! I am sick of you being so damn sure of your opinions. All you men are the same—so sure you know what is going on!

KENNETH: Well, I am not like every man. I think I've gotten to know you pretty well, and like most women I know, you take the men in your life for granted. And now you accuse me of being like every other man, even though I have given you every consideration!

LEANNE: Well, I have Michelle's back here. Kenneth, I think you are out of line. Who made you the expert on marriage? It sounds like your marriage has its challenges, too! I'm with Michelle—men sometimes are just so arrogant!

KYLE: Well, I have to say that I can see where Kenneth is coming from. It does seem that the women in this group have a tendency to complain about their partners.

DAISY: I'm aware of some stereotyping of each other happening in the group. I'm wondering what that is about. When a group member says that another group member is like all men or all women, it feels like there is something going on in the group, because usually we are much more personal than that with each other. Does anybody have any thoughts or feelings about what may be going on in the group?

[A short period of silence]

SHEILA: This is a risky thing to say, but I have felt that Kenneth and Michelle have been flirting the last few months, and I've been feeling a little jealous about it. In a way I was feeling glad to see them fight! This is super embarrassing to say, but—now I've said it!

KYLE: Come to think of it, I have picked up on some energy between those two! But I felt disappointed to see them fight.

KENNETH: Okay, yes, I do think that Michelle is attractive, I won't deny it! I wish I had the kind of aliveness in my marriage that we have here. I mean here we can be honest. My wife and I never talk!

MICHELLE: Thank you for your honesty, Kenneth. That feels a lot better than being judged. I'm too tired to be attracted to anybody to tell you the truth, but I love the honesty.

SIMON: Well, as the only gay man in this group, I feel a little left out of this hetero-centric discussion, but I feel we are getting closer in the group, and it probably makes us all feel a little uncomfortable at times. I agree with Kenneth that it would be nice to have the kind of honesty out in the real world that we have in here!

DAISY: Any other feelings about what is happening between us?

The group discussion continued for some time. The name-calling between Michelle and Kenneth stopped, and the group was able to resume a more contactful mode of interacting.

Note that I turned the discussion to the group-as-a-whole by making a few simple observations, not by making a grand interpretation. This is very much in keeping with gestalt therapy's phenomenological attitude, in which it is much more the therapist's role to meet the client in dialogue than it is to interpret the client's experience. Putting on the group-as-a-whole lens begins with a simple shift in the leader's perspective—the leader feels into perceiving the group as one might imagine viewing a family as a system at the family dinner table. Making contact with the group flows naturally from that simple shift of foreground focus.

Another aspect of working with the shifting foreground focus relates to the question of when to keep an interpersonal group process in the foreground and when to let issues from group members' lives outside the group come into focus. To put it differently: there are times when the GGT leader will want to keep the focus in the room, and request that group members work only with what is occurring between group members. At other times, the GGT leader will want to attend to issues in group members' lives outside of the group, such as those pertaining to personal history, relationships, work, life goals, and so on. Finding a pleasing balance between "inside-the-group-room" and "outside-the-group-room" is an important skill for GGT leaders. Each GGT leader will have their own approach to finding the right balance point.

At times in all of our groups we will say something to this effect: "Imagine that there is a circle, a boundary around the group right now. Let's spend the next 45 minutes just attending to what is happening between us. We will come back to the concerns of our outside lives later, but for now, let's just attend to how things feel in the room and any feelings that group members may have toward each other or toward the leaders. Anything is fair game as long as it concerns our group and the relationships between us." When we say this, it consistently raises the energy level in the group. If people are dozing off, they almost always wake up when we shift the foreground focus in this way.

When the focus is overly weighted in the direction of group members' lives outside the group, the emotional range between group members tends to become restricted and limited to positive, supportive feedback. While helpful and important, such feedback does not have the range, risk, and emotional force of more engaged interpersonal processing that will stimulate intense emotions such as attraction, envy, anger, or hurt. On the other hand, when the group is overly weighted on interpersonal processing in the room, the group can generate more heat than light. When this occurs, group members can get caught in group melodrama that serves to keep members occupied but fails to promote awareness and insight. In GGT we want neither saccharine sweetness nor to become a tempest in a teapot. Instead, we search for a balance in which group members may experience intense emotions toward each other and also have the support necessary to generalize their learning in group to their everyday lives.

Conclusion

In this chapter we have sought to give gestalt group therapists some tools to deal with common difficulties that arise in the group: a difficult group member, scapegoating, and conflict between members in the group. The tools we described all involve thinking and feeling into the group as a living, functioning system. We have also sought to give gestalt group therapists some tools to help maintain a good, positive flow of energy in the group. We have suggested that when there is difficulty in the group, it is often best to turn the therapist's focus to the group-as-a-whole. When there is smooth sailing, work at the individual level will often be the best choice. When the gestalt group therapist has developed the skills to shift the focus of her attention back and forth between the individuals in the group and the group-as-a-whole, she has vastly increased her range of available interventions in creating a group that can sustain over time and foster growth and change in each of its members.

References

Beck, A. P. (1981a). A study of group phase development and emergent leadership. *Group*, 5(4), 48–54.

Beck, A. P. (1981b). Developmental characteristics of the system-forming process. In J. E. Durkin (Ed.), *Living groups: Group psychotherapy and general system theory*. New York: Brunner/Mazel.

Ronall, R. (2008). Intensive gestalt workshops: Experiences in community. In B. Feder & J. Frew (Eds), *Beyond the hot seat revisited: Gestalt approaches to group* (pp. 217–243). New Orleans, LA: Gestalt Institute Press.

Yalom, I. D., & Leszcz, M. (2005). *Theory and practice of group psychotherapy*. New York: Basic Books.

Chapter 8

Traditional Gestalt Therapy Groups
Individual-level Work at the Foreground

This chapter is written in the voices of both Peter and Daisy

In GGT our core mission is the growth and development of each individual group member. In earlier chapters we have discussed the group process and how working with the group-as-a-whole helps foster this growth. In this chapter, we are going to turn our focus to individual pieces of work with the leader. Work of this type has a long and storied history in gestalt therapy. Readers who are gestalt therapists will likely be very familiar with this style of working, but for group therapists who have not been exposed to traditional gestalt therapy groups, we hope in this chapter to give you a flavor of how traditionally run gestalt groups operate and foster growth.

Working one-on-one with the leader, exploring a "piece of work" can be an amazing and transformative experience. This we know from personal experience, having logged in many hours as clients working one-on-one with our gestalt mentors in the company of gestalt groups. Although formal attention to individual pieces of work in succession is not the modality we typically choose for our current work, we return to highly focused individual pieces of work regularly. There is an aesthetic beauty and clarity of purpose to a traditionally run gestalt group that is unique in our experience. The group members are present for support and witnessing. The method of promoting growth is not the group process, but the interaction between the leader and the group member in the "hot seat" or "open seat." Fritz Perls first made this modality famous in workshops designed not to create a new method of group therapy, but as a way to demonstrate one-on-one gestalt therapy to professionals. These original, classical gestalt demonstrations transformed over time into a methodology that grew in popularity because they were a very effective and powerful vehicle for personal growth.

Part of what makes GGT distinct from other forms of group therapy is an underlying appreciation for the value of one-on-one intensive work that can unfold between the group leader and an individual group member. When we, the authors, present our work at the American Group Psychotherapy Association to group therapists who have not been exposed to GGT, workshop attendees are often surprised by the depth that we will go into as group facilitators with one group member. Even when we are working in an interactive group process modality, we are open to shifting the focus to an individual piece of work that comes up. Typically, a "piece of work" may last around 20 minutes.

The gestalt group leader will often bring the following to the one-on-one piece of work:

• Focusing on the contact between the group leader and the group member
• Engaging with the client in the spirit of dialogue
• Suggesting an experiment that supports the group member's awareness and growth
• Supporting the group member's integration of what they have experienced

In a traditional gestalt group (please note that we are not using the term "gestalt group therapy" here, which we reserve for the interactive style), the group typically begins with a "check-in."[1] The check-in is an opportunity for each member to say something about what he or she is thinking and feeling, to share anything that they would like the group to know about, and to say something about what they might want to work on for that day. At times, the leader will have a very brief interaction with each group member who is checking in. The purpose of this interaction is typically to provide a moment that might help support each group member's awareness. Here is a typical example:

GRACE: I'll check in. My mother came to visit this weekend from out of town, and I feel like I turned to ice inside! [Makes a fist with her hand] She is so intrusive! She says the most insensitive things to me—always inquiring about the things I am most sensitive about, like my relationships, and if I'm lonely! Yes, I'm lonely, but I will never tell her about that! She has no idea where she ends and I begin!

DAISY: Grace, would you try doing that hand gesture again? [Daisy does the hand gesture herself to point it out to Grace] But this time, exaggerate it just a little and add words to it—see if you can articulate in words what your hand is saying.

GRACE: [Makes the fist again, a little more forcefully this time] This woman will never let up on me. When I tell her to back off, she collapses into a puddle on the floor, so the only thing I can do is curl up into a cold little ice cube.

DAISY: What do you feel in your body and in your emotions as you say that?

GRACE: Oh, that is easy—I feel so angry, but also so helpless, because nothing I have ever done has ever changed her. In my body I feel frozen, like an ice queen.

DAISY: Okay, thanks. This sounds like there might be something to explore here. Maybe something to work on today?

GRACE: Yes, we'll see if I can thaw enough to work on it! [Group members smile and softly laugh supportively]

DAISY: I suspect you can Grace; you've already started! Are you checked in for now?

GRACE: Yes, for now.

CHUCK: Well, I can check in. I'm doing okay, I guess. I keep thinking about the homeless people I work with and I'm thinking, "there but for the grace of God go I." Of course, I'm not much of a believer in God—but still I feel that. It just makes me so angry the way society throws these people out. Nobody gives a shit about them.

PETER: I am touched by your identification with them, Chuck. Can you say a bit about how you feel right now, reflecting on this?

CHUCK: I feel lost. Like I'm in the jungle and I've lost my map, compass, GPS, —you name it.

PETER: Sounds scary.

CHUCK: It would be if it were not so familiar. I'm like a stranger in a strange land. I'm used to it. So, no, I wouldn't say that I'm scared, just out here on my own.

PETER: And here and now with the group, how does it feel to be with us in this moment, sharing your experience?

CHUCK: [Takes a moment to look around, make some eye contact, and take a few deep breaths] It feels better. More grounded.

PETER: More connected?

CHUCK: Yes, that too. Okay, thanks—I'm checked in. I may want to reserve some time to work on these feelings later today.

PETER: Sounds good—I would like that!

Discussion of the Check-in

Each group member is sharing enough of themselves to provide the group with a small glimpse into their state of mind, body, spirit, or situation.

Typically, group members will not interrupt each other's check-in; however, there is a great deal of connection and eye contact between group members during the check-in. Each person's check-in will typically last about five minutes or so. Part of its purpose is to give each member a chance to connect the group with how they are doing in the moment, while concurrently using the presence of the group to gather awareness of their feelings. A further purpose of the check-in is for the group leader to gain a sense of who would like to do a piece of work during a given group session. Part of the work of leadership in a traditional gestalt group is time management, in that every group member will not have an opportunity to do a piece of work every group session. Therefore, it is important that the leader keeps track of time, and from session to session to ensure that all group members have ample opportunities for their work.

Chuck does a Piece of Work with Peter

In this section we will explore how a piece of work can unfold with the leader in traditional gestalt therapy. After the check-in, the leader will typically ask the group if someone is ready to do a piece of work. If there are co-leaders (as we, your authors, usually are), once the group member comes forward we will ask which of the co-leaders he or she prefers to work with.

In the first one-on-one session we will describe, Chuck, who checked in a few paragraphs earlier, comes forward and decides to work with Peter. We will provide some background on Chuck's story so that you, the reader, will have a better context for understanding this piece of work. It is important to note that group members know Chuck's story, because they have been in group with him for some time, and this knowledge of his history builds empathy and compassion between group members.

Chuck grew up in Johnstown, Pennsylvania, in the 1950s and 1960s. He is an African American gay man whose dad worked as a janitor in a steel mill. His mother was a housekeeper who worked for the family of a manager at the same steel mill. He was the youngest of three siblings, with two older sisters. Chuck was 60 when he started to work with Peter, individually. He was married and had one son and three grandchildren. He had spent his career working for the county government as a social worker, doing case work with chronically mentally ill and homeless people, and had retired several years prior to this group session.

When Chuck was 18 years old, he was drafted and shipped off to Vietnam. He served in the 101st Airborne Division and was wounded in the battle of "Hamburger Hill," where he lost three fingers of his left hand and suffered other injuries that left him with chronic nerve pain. He was hospitalized for several months in Germany, and was eventually honorably discharged from the military. He returned home to Johnstown but did not get along with his family after the war. An army buddy lived in the Sacramento area, and invited Chuck to room with him there, so he came to California and went to college on the GI Bill where he earned a BA and Master's in Social Work at Sacramento State University. From Sacramento State, he went on to a county social work position, where he worked for many years.

Chuck entered therapy because of depression, conflict about his sexuality, and post-traumatic stress from his war trauma. Although he was in a long-term heterosexual marriage, he and his wife were not sexual with each other, and he frequented gay bath-houses in the San Francisco Bay Area. Although he had come out to his wife, he had not come out to his son or to his community, and as far as he knew, his son, grandchildren, friends, and members of his church were unaware that he was gay. Chuck's passion was working with the homeless mentally ill, and especially homeless vets with whom he greatly identified.

Through the course of therapy, Chuck made the choice to come out to his son, who turned out to be loving and supportive. Chuck's church community was another matter. Its members turned against him. He left that faith community behind and has not found a new one. Chuck and his wife were now separated but remained friends. The following piece of work is somewhat abbreviated.

CHUCK: I'm thinking about my check-in. Every time I pass a homeless person on the street—which seems like every five minutes these days—there are so many here in Sacramento—I get this pang, this horrible, lost feeling. I think about coming home from Vietnam as a vet, and a black vet at that, and I can tell you, nobody wanted you. You were worse than invisible; you were like the garbage that smells bad and everybody wants to throw out.

PETER: Over the years as you've shared this trauma with me and given me the opportunity to be with you in hearing your experience, one of the things that always surprises me is that it's not the experience of war, or of being injured, that you keep coming back to. It's the experience of coming home and being rejected by your community.

CHUCK: Not just my community. It was my family too. They were so caught up in their own lives that no one hardly noticed that I came home from the war! I mean, they were sympathetic about the injury to my hand, but that was it! Nobody asked about my experiences over there. Nobody asked how I was doing, or even if I was in pain.

PETER: What are you aware of in your body, as you say this right now?

CHUCK: I'm back to that "stranger in a strange land" feeling. Like I'm totally lost and on the verge of panic.

PETER: Okay, let's just stay with that feeling and see if we can be with it together.

CHUCK: It's a feeling in my head, like I'm swimming in a murky sea. I can't see anything. I don't know if I'm up or down.

PETER: Okay, I am with you. Please pay attention to your breath, and let's see what happens in your body and your awareness.

CHUCK: This is how I felt coming home. I was a triple threat to society, and believe me, nobody wanted to deal with that!

PETER: A triple threat?

CHUCK: Black, a vet who saw what America was really up to over there, and gay. I mean, believe you me, I fit in exactly nowhere!

PETER: And what do you feel right now?

CHUCK: Angry as hell! Just angry as hell!

PETER: I like feeling your anger. I can feel your power now! Is there anyone in particular your anger feels directed at right now?

CHUCK: Well, there is my dad, and he was a man who went through a hell of a lot as a black man in his time, so I don't like to blame him. And also, he's long dead, so there's really no point.

PETER: The point certainly would not be to blame him for anything. The point would be to explore your feelings. If we were to put him in the empty chair, and you were to express your feelings to him, do you think you could give yourself permission to express your anger, but also hold that you may have many other, positive feelings toward him?

CHUCK: Yes, I think I could do that. He was not a bad man! He worked his ass off for us kids!

PETER: I get that! And I also get that you are allowed to have complicated feelings toward your father! Most people do!

CHUCK: Okay.

[Daisy pulls out an empty chair]

PETER: Okay, Chuck, please take a moment and imagine your father sitting in the empty chair, and, at the same time, support your anger—that feeling in your body that you know is your anger—and tell him about your anger.

CHUCK: [Tears are flowing] Dad, you were a good provider for us, but you had no idea what I've gone through in life. Do you have any idea what it is like to come home from a shitty war, to be so fucked up, and to have your father never even give you a hug or tell you he is proud of you? Do you know what that is like? It is devastating! That is what it is like! It tears you apart from the inside. That is why I left and came out to California. Nobody was going to see the real me at home! So I took care of myself! On my own! Fuck! I didn't want to leave! You sent me away by ignoring me!

PETER: You are doing beautifully. I am right here with you, and I believe the group is, too. How did he do with you being gay? Would you talk to him about that?

CHUCK: [Without missing a beat and staring right at the chair as if his dad was there] Dad, if you had paid one bit of attention to me, you would have seen I was gay! There were lots of gay black men in Johnstown. They were in the closet, but they were there, and you knew plenty of them! You always made mean, sick jokes about them behind their backs. You had nothing but contempt for gay people, and especially gay black people! If I had told you about how I felt, about my sexuality, you would have turned that contempt on me. And I couldn't handle that! I needed your respect! I could never be true to myself as long as you were alive! You made my life impossible!

PETER: You are standing on your own ground. Just exactly your own ground. How do you feel in your body and your emotions?

CHUCK: I feel good. Damn good. It feels good to finally tell him the truth of my life. There are a few more things I want to tell him.

PETER: Go for it!

CHUCK: I married Janice just so that you and Mom would approve of me. There was no other reason. I was living a lie. And God-damn it, you still never gave me your approval! What a waste! I am over living in the closet, Dad. I do not live that way anymore. I am proud of who I am, so you can take your homophobia to your grave. I'm over it!

PETER: Is there anything else that you want to say to him before we put the empty chair away?

CHUCK: Yes. I know that racist America fucked you over, Dad. You were a good provider. I know that cleaning up that steel mill day after day and all the shit you took was an incredible burden. You gave me life and put food on our table every day. I will always be grateful for that. So fuck you for being a homophobic jerk who never even hugged me after coming home from Vietnam, but thank you for being a good provider for our family.

PETER: Let's just take a moment to come back to your body and emotions. What are you feeling?

CHUCK: I'm tingling —feeling shook up, but strong. Like something that has been a long time coming has finally found expression! I am getting that I can love him and hate what he has done to my life. That is a new feeling for me.

PETER: Okay. Thank you.

CHUCK: Thank you!

After a piece of work is completed, the leader will ask the group member whether he or she is up for some sharing from group members. Sharing in this context is very different from sharing or feedback in an interactive group process context. After a group member has done an intense, one-on-one piece of work with the leader, then sharing from the group is generally limited to "I-statements" from other group members, sharing feelings that came up for them during the individual work, and bringing the focus back to the group member who has worked. The group leader will generally ask that sharing exclude any insights about the person who has done the piece of work, or any continuation of the work, as tempting as those insights or suggestions might be to share. The reasons for keeping the sharing focused in this way are that the person who has just worked has typically had a very intense experience, and the group is relying on the expertise of the leader and that member together in gauging when they have reached an optimal stopping point for the present time. The group member who has just done a piece of work is typically very opened up at this point, having perhaps tried something emotionally challenging. Their fixed gestalts may be disrupted as new creative adjustments are emerging. Old defenses may be down, and the group member is therefore particularly vulnerable. So, the leader's main job during the sharing is to keep the group member safe from over-stimulation from other group members at this point.

Here is a share after Chuck's work offered by Jenny, a 28-year-old group member:

JENNY: When you spoke at the end of the work about your being angry with your father at the same time that you really respect him for the support he gave your family, that meant a lot to me. It is hard for me to be angry with my mom, but also hold on to the fact that I really love her and am a very loyal daughter. So that was awesome. I was also moved by your sharing about coming home from Vietnam. You know I am too young to really understand all that was involved in that war, but I thank you for your service. It means a lot that you did what you did and sacrificed, so I was very appreciative. [Tearing up] My dad served over there. He never talked about it, so it means a lot to hear you share. As you know, he's an alcoholic, and I'm sure the war played a big part in all of that, so your work means a lot to me. I feel a lot closer to you than before. Thank you.

When other group members have shared their personal reflections with the group member who has done their work, then the group leader asks who is ready to do the next piece of work.

Grace, whose check-in we shared at the beginning of this chapter, says that she is ready to step up and do a piece of work. Her preferred therapist for today is Daisy. First, let us share a bit about Grace, so that you, the reader, will come to know her story as group members have.

Grace is 35 years old. She is quite thin, with red hair, and has an intense, often sad, look on her face. She looks and feels a little brittle. She is the older of two girls, born into a wealthy white family in suburban Detroit, Michigan. Her father is a highly successful radiologist and her mother is a homemaker. She had moved out to the San Francisco Bay Area for graduate school in order to study psychology and stayed after her Master's degree. Having completed her licensing hours, Grace is now in the beginning phase of setting up a private practice. She has been in individual therapy for several years with a colleague of ours who specializes in eating disorders. Grace has been dealing with an eating disorder since she was hospitalized at age 15 suffering from anorexia. Her eating and compulsive exercising are under good control with weekly therapy.

Grace identifies as heterosexual. She has had several relationships, but none that have lasted more than two years. An ongoing theme for Grace is confluence and conflict in her relationship with her mother, along with a strong desire to please her demanding and perfectionistic father, whom she feels is disappointed that she did not attend medical school.

DAISY: I'm so glad you chose to do a piece of work today, Grace!

GRACE: It feels a little risky. I have been pretty frozen. I get this way when my mother visits.

DAISY: Okay. Let's see if we can be with your frozen state together.

GRACE: Hmmm ... I don't know if you really want to go there!

DAISY: Oh yes, I really do—I want you to have me with you in this space. So, let's start with your body experience.

GRACE: I am stiff, cold. Nobody can get to me because there is a block of ice between me and them.

DAISY: That sounds very sad, Grace! Is the block of ice between you and me?

GRACE: [Slows down to check in with herself] No, I don't feel the ice between me and you. It's between me and the rest of the world.

DAISY: I am so glad to be with you—on your team, so to speak!

GRACE: It's weird to have you here. I'm used to shutting women out, especially women who are old enough to be my mother!

DAISY: What sort of weird?

GRACE: It feels a little overwhelming, like I'm an ice sculpture and you might break or melt me.

DAISY: Thank you so much for letting me know! I do want to be on your team, to be on your side of the block of ice that separates you from people, but I hear that I have to be very mindful of how we are doing together. Fortunately, we have time, both today and in our ongoing work together here in the group, to find the right way for me to be with you. [Pauses and holds a moment of silence] How might I break you or melt you?

GRACE: You could make it all about you! Or you could abandon me! Or you could say something awful to me! My mom did all of these things to me all the time.

DAISY: Those things do sound awful. I'm sorry you had to go through that. Is there more you might want to tell me about her?

GRACE: Thank you—yes. Well, one of the hardest things was that she was so unstable. She had a pretty severe alcohol problem, and she would constantly threaten suicide. It was horrible. I was constantly terrified that she was going to kill herself. And she did make a few pretty serious attempts; she was hospitalized, I think, five times during my childhood. So, yeah, I am pretty wary.

DAISY: It sounds like you have been through hell with her, Grace. I am very impressed with you—that you haven't broken or melted into a puddle! I think you have a remarkable resilience! Let's focus back in on us. How are you feeling, right here and now, between you and me?

GRACE: I feel pretty good. Pretty safe. So far you have been okay.

DAISY: I want you to let me know when I get it wrong with you!

GRACE: Yes, I will try—that is a big risk for me. My mom had no room for that kind of thing! It was all about me taking care of her!

DAISY: Yes, right. I hear that! You know I think the group might support you if you take some risks with me. Say you were hurt by something I had done—I think the group could really help you talk to me!

GRACE: Oh boy, now things are getting hot! There is something, but I have not had the nerve to talk with you about it. I can feel my heart starting to race!

DAISY: Okay, well, let's take our time with this. Is there anyone in the group who might be a support for you in talking with me about this? I want you to have lots of support! Please look around the room and see who might be a strong support for you.

GRACE: Wow—that sounds so amazing—to have support! Well, Chuck, I just heard your piece of work and I really have grown to trust you! I would be so grateful to have you have my back here.

CHUCK: I would love to do it, Grace!

DAISY: Would it be okay for Chuck to come sit next to you, Grace? Would that be okay with you, Chuck?

[Chuck sits next to Grace, and she takes his hand as she confronts Daisy]

GRACE: Well, this began several months ago, Daisy, and I was so hurt, and I just didn't know what to do about it.

DAISY: I am right here, Grace. I want to know about how I've hurt you.

GRACE: It has happened in group a number of times, and it is hard to talk about. But I felt very ashamed and dismissed.

DAISY: Those are terrible feelings to have, and I am so glad you are talking to me about it!

GRACE: Well, it has to do with my participation in the group. It feels like you reach out to other people, but never to me! Like I could sit here forever, and you would never ask how I am doing! And this feels so shameful and ridiculous to say!

DAISY: It's not ridiculous at all, Grace. Before I respond, I just want to ask you to take a moment to feel Chuck's support.

[Grace makes eye contact with Chuck and a sense of support is conveyed non-verbally]

DAISY: I hear that I have failed to reach out to you, Grace, and I am so glad you have brought that to my attention! I would never want to ignore you! Can you tell me more about it?

GRACE: Well, sometimes when people say things in group, you will interact with them a bit, offering thoughts, insight, or an experiment. But not so much with me! Maybe once in a while you'll respond, but not a lot! And I end up feeling like you don't like me!

[Grace cries, and a group member hands her a tissue in a show of support]

DAISY: Is there more I need to know? I feel so pleased that we can talk about this!

GRACE: Well, I want to know why. Do you have any idea why you ignore me?

DAISY: I really was not aware of this until now, Grace. It definitely was not my intention to ignore you! As I think about it, maybe I have the feeling that I will say the wrong thing, rub you the wrong way, and so I have held back.

GRACE: Do you feel that I over-react to you?

DAISY: No, not at all. I am just trying to respond honestly to your question. I think it is important, because I want to work on our relationship so that we can be in good contact.

GRACE: Well, I know I am sensitive—always on the lookout for something negative. But really, I think you are pretty safe for me. I don't want you to hold back. Even if I object to what you say, I would much rather have you reach out to me.

DAISY: Okay. Thank you so much for taking this risk with me. I feel so good about us getting into better alignment. And, yes, I will try to be aware of this tendency to hold back with you. I don't want to do that!

GRACE: Okay. Thank you!

DAISY: How does it feel to assert yourself with me and to get your needs met?

GRACE: It feels new, scary—I'm flushed all over!

DAISY: And what about the block of ice?

GRACE: Oh, my gosh—I forgot about that! No block of ice at the moment.

DAISY: And how is that, to have the ice gone away for the moment?

GRACE: Liberating, loose, free.

DAISY: Does this feel like an okay stopping place?

GRACE: Yes. Thank you, Chuck, for your support. You were great!

CHUCK: I'm so glad to see you stand up for yourself, Grace!

DAISY: Grace, how would some sharing from the rest of the group be?

GRACE: I'd like that!

[Group members then share their feedback with Grace]

Conclusion

One thing we would like the reader to notice in these two vignettes, Peter with Chuck and Daisy with Grace, is that the two of us worked quite differently from each other—each meeting our client on the distinct "narrow ridge" (Buber, 1992, p. 40) that is a meeting in time and place, between person and person. Laura Perls ([1992] 2012, p. 140) states that,

> *a Gestalt therapist does not use techniques: he applies himself in and to a situation with whatever professional skill and life experience he has accumulated and integrated. There are as many styles as there are therapists and clients who discover themselves and each other and together invent their relationship.*

Gestalt therapy supports each gestalt therapist in being and expressing him or herself in the therapy—bringing forth their unique talents, perspectives, and ways of relating with clients. Of course, expressing oneself as a therapist is not license to do whatever one pleases; instead, the therapist finds freedom of expression supported by the container of sound theory and methodology.

We hope in this chapter to have given you, the reader, a sense of what traditional gestalt groups look and feel like. Even now, as we have adopted the interactive style of GGT, we return from time to time to this traditional format. Also, as we mentioned earlier, the aesthetic of this format, the intensity and depth of one-on-one contact, often punctuated by experiment, permeates GGT's interactive style, making room for the leader to focus on the individual when such focus feels like a sound choice for the group.

Note

1 When running interactive GGT, we typically do not begin with a check-in, but if the focus in a particular session will be on individual pieces of work, then we may start with a check-in.

References

Buber, M. (1992). *On intersubjectivity and cultural creativity*. Chicago, IL: University of Chicago Press.
Perls, L. (1992). *Living at the boundary*. Gouldsboro, ME: Gestalt Journal Press.

Chapter 9

A Sample Gestalt Group Therapy Session

This chapter is written in the voices of both Peter and Daisy

In this chapter, our goal is to give you a sense of how a GGT session feels, from beginning to end. We typically work in the interactive GGT mode described in this chapter. In Chapter 8, our purpose was to convey a sense of how traditional gestalt groups work. As we said there, the aesthetic of traditional gestalt groups lives on in modern, interactive GGT, as we often move into deep one-on-one work when we feel it is appropriate. So we want you, the reader, to have a sense of both the traditional and interactive approaches, as there can be no modern, interactive GGT without the history of traditional gestalt therapy.

The GGT group described in this chapter meets every other week for an hour and a half. Additionally, the group meets twice a year for a day-long session. The group we present here is an hour and a half session. Two members happen to be transitioning out of group during this session.

One difficulty in presenting a GGT session in print is that trying to keep each person's story straight can be confusing. This is not a problem at all in the real life of a GGT group wherein each person and their history are felt distinctively and viscerally. We have written a brief sketch of each group member and suggest that you, the reader, refer back to these sketches if you lose track of who is who when reading through the give and take of the GGT session. First, we'll give a paragraph of background on the two group members who are leaving the group. We then give a quick introduction to the four members who are staying.

> Mara [leaving] is a 45-year-old Jewish lesbian who is a social worker in private practice. Mara has been in the group for three years, and has decided to leave it after meeting many of her life goals, among which were to shift from working in a high stress job at a women's shelter to a private practice, and to find and sustain a more fulfilling intimate relationship. Mara tends to be introverted, and originally had been rather emotionally distant and self-protective in the group.

Her parents' divorce when she was eight was ugly and contentious. Her father went on to quickly remarry and have two children with his new wife. Mara feels that her father gave more love, attention, and resources to his new family than he did to her. Mara's mother also remarried and had children with her new husband. Mara often felt alone as a child. These feelings came up in group as well. Her fixed relational gestalts in the group centered around a tendency to feel like an outsider, to stay emotionally disengaged from other group members, and to feel wary of the group leaders. In the first year or so of group, she would say little, and needed quite a bit of support in order to share her thoughts and feelings. Over time, she opened up significantly. With group support, she was able to mobilize herself to leave an unsatisfying relationship and begin a far more gratifying one. She left her job at the shelter and took the leap into private practice. She now feels that it is a good time to leave group, having moved forward in these two important areas of her life.

Mark [leaving] is a 50-year-old straight, white administrator with the federal government. He is married to a woman he has been in a relationship with for 20 years. One of Mark's main goals in coming into group was to speak up for himself more fully in his marriage. He and his wife had been in a significant amount of conflict around a variety of issues, and Mark had a tendency to internalize anger about the way he was being treated by his wife. When Mark was in early childhood, his father abandoned the family. His mom worked at low-paying jobs, and Mark grew up knowing poverty and sometimes hunger. He grew up very devoted to his mother. In group, Mark had at first been highly attuned to other people's needs and was quite disconnected with himself. When speaking of his own needs, he would become highly intellectual and abstract. Over time, he received feedback from group members that, when he spoke clearly and unambiguously about his needs, he was much easier to relate to, and felt more emotionally available to group members. He was now leaving the group, feeling that after five years he was better able to stand up for himself, and that he was more satisfied with his marriage and relationship with his adult children.

Rosario [staying] is a 35-year-old straight Latina who works in a public school teaching third grade. She is single.

Amy [staying] is a straight, 40-year-old citizen of Singapore, a psychologist who is a university professor. She is working with a green card.

Raj [staying] is a 75-year-old straight, Indian-American psychiatrist who is retired.

Sharon [staying] is a straight, 70-year-old Jewish marriage and family therapist who is in private practice.

When people join any of our ongoing groups, we ask that they commit to staying in the group initially for at least six months, and that they stay for four sessions after announcing that they are leaving the group, so that group members have time to say goodbye to them, and they in turn have a chance to fully process saying goodbye too. These commitments are especially important in an interactive GGT format, where the emphasis is highly relational, with a major focus on the relationships that form between group members. When a group member leaves, it is a major event in the life of the group that requires time and attention.

In this group, two group members had decided to leave, and they coordinated their leaving so that they were leaving on the same date. This was their last session. New members were scheduled to begin at the following session. We have abbreviated what a full session would entail, but have brought out many of the salient pieces to help give a flavor of the session.

DAISY: Let's begin the session with some centering. Please close your eyes and pay attention to your body and your breathing. Notice any points of tension and just breathe into those places. When you are ready, open your eyes, and come into the room. When opening your eyes, try staying centered in your own experience as you begin to make visual contact with other group members.

(Please note that, with interactive GGT, we do not begin with a formal check-in as we do in the traditional format. Generally, each person will get their voice into the room, but with less formality than occurs with a check-in.)

SHARON: I am aware of the fact that the anniversary of my dad's death was last week. He's been gone for 15 years now! Can you believe it? [Looks at Daisy, who has been working with her in a combination of individual and group therapy since before her father died]
DAISY: Wow, 15 years!
SHARON: Time flies when you are having fun!
DAISY: I'm appreciating how long we've been working together, and what a rich experience that has been! When you think about your dad, how do you feel, Sharon?
SHARON: Oh, I miss him terribly. I light a yahrzeit candle every year for him. He was the best! The last years were hard, because he was so sick and not himself, but I really miss him!
AMY: I'm so glad you had him, and that he was there for you, Sharon. And I love the Jewish tradition of lighting the yahrzeit candle. My

dad is still alive, but I never really got much of anything from him, so I have a different kind of grief. It is the grief of being neglected in my childhood. I feel envious of what you had with him!

SHARON: I hear that your dad was not there for you, Amy. I'm sorry about that. And yes, I was lucky, and I do miss him terribly!

RAJ: As you ladies are speaking of your fathers, I can't help but identify with them. I am getting older, and I am in good health, but I know that cannot last forever. I feel that my death is not very far off.

AMY: Don't say that, Raj! I've gotten way too attached to you to let you go!

RAJ: Thank you, Amy! I'll do my best to stick around! Amy, you mentioned last session that you are dating—how is your new relationship going?

AMY: Oh, I don't want to jinx it, but it is going well! We are going slow, which is new for me, but I like him! I like him a lot!

[Everyone in the room looks very interested in Amy's new relationship and happy for her]

DAISY: I am really glad you are doing this in a new way, Amy—a way that feels right for you!

AMY: Yes, this really is new. I typically go into a new relationship at break-neck speed, and things have gotten away from me. Relationships have all gone bad; I'm trying to be more conscious this time.

RAJ: Amy, I know that dating has not been easy for you. I'm glad you are feeling good about where things are with him!

AMY: Thank you, Raj! All my dad does is criticize me: comment on my body, criticize my weight. It feels good to have your support.

RAJ: I think this young man is very lucky to be dating you!

AMY: Well, thank you! I like him. It is scary, though. I've had a lot of disappointments.

RAJ: Hang in there!

AMY: I will try!

PETER: We are talking about forming relationships, and also about death. I'm aware that we have two endings here in the group, with this being Mara's and Mark's last day. We have spent a lot of time and emotional energy in getting attached and connected to each other—and now we are coming to this parting. How are people feeling about this?

MARK: I have been listening to Buddhist teachings called "Dharma Talks" on podcasts, and there is a lot of discussion about non-attachment. I am really working on letting go—being non-attached. So, I totally appreciate all you guys and all you have done for me, but at the same time, I'm working on letting go. I feel that it is the right time for me to go.

PETER: I just want to say to both of you, Mark and Mara, that you are leaving in a way that feels very respectful to the group and our process. You've stuck around for the four sessions to let us take our time with saying goodbye. That means a lot to me and I want you to know that I appreciate it. It's a big deal for us to get connected and attached to each other in here. We carry each other around—internalize each other—and it takes a respectful process to bring that to a close. You both are really honoring that!

MARK: You know I have said before that I don't think about the group in-between sessions, but I've been really thinking about that, and I've come to realize that that is not exactly true. I actually do carry you guys around with me. Since we've been talking about that, I've noticed it more—become more aware of carrying you guys with me. And having you "with me" has helped me out in the world—in my life. I'm much more able to speak up for myself with my wife, and also at work. I've learned to speak more directly. I carry you guys with me when I do that!

MARA: I want to say, too, that leaving feels hard, but I think it is the right decision for now. You guys have seen me through a lot of change! I was pretty depressed when I started out with the group, but I learned, kind of like Mark, how to speak up more for myself. And I don't know if I really could have handled the kind of intimacy I have in my new relationship if I hadn't learned how to talk about my feelings in here.

SHARON: You have really been amazing, Mara! The changes you have been through in here have been pretty remarkable: new, better job; new, better relationship. I'm going to miss you. And you too, Mark. Too much loss for me! I'm really going to miss you guys. [Tears up] I don't do well with loss.

PETER: I think you are doing quite well with it, Sharon. You are expressing your feelings, not pushing the feelings away. I'd say that is a pretty good way to deal with loss!

SHARON: I feel such a yearning for my dad. He was such a special person. It does feel good to talk about it, and to say goodbye to you guys, Mara and Mark. You have been important to me!

MARA: You've meant a lot to me too, Sharon. I'll miss all of you guys!

DAISY: Rosario, I notice that you have been quiet so far this session. Just wanting to check in with you.

ROSARIO: This is really hard for me. You know my story! My mom died when I was two, and my aunt and uncle brought me up. I never even knew my dad. So when people leave, I just withdraw. Part of me feels like crawling up into a ball.

RAJ: I know you had terrible losses when you were little, Rosario. I did too. I just want you to know that I am really here with you.

ROSARIO: That means a lot, Raj! I don't mean to feel sorry for myself.

DAISY: You are letting us be with you with what you are feeling, Rosario. We can't ask for more than that.

ROSARIO: [To Mark] It has been good getting to know you! I think you have changed a lot since you started. At first, I could barely understand you at times, you talked around the things you meant to say. Now you really say what you mean! I think it is great. And Mara, I'm so glad you have found the love of your life! You've been an inspiration to me—making changes—changes are hard for me—and you've made lots of them.

MARA: I'm going to really miss you too, Rosario!

ROSARIO: It just makes me sad, though. I think about my cousins and my aunt and uncle. They love me like a sister, like a daughter, but sometimes I can't help feeling like I've been a burden to them. They were not wealthy people. It was not an easy thing to take in another kid—an unexpected kid—and put food on the table for me. Sometimes I just feel like a burden.

DAISY: Does that feeling come up for you in here, Rosario?

ROSARIO: Well, I know this isn't rational, but I guess I feel that maybe part of the reason these guys are leaving group is because I have been such a drain on the group emotionally with my problems.

DAISY: This takes a lot of courage to bring this up, Rosario; I am very impressed! Let me encourage you to check it out with them.

ROSARIO: Don't you think they would just lie?

DAISY: I don't know. Why don't you make some contact with Mark or Mara and see what happens?

ROSARIO: [To Mark] I know this sounds crazy, Mark, but I want to know if I have been a burden or a drag to be with in group? Have I driven you away?

MARK: I'm really glad you asked, Rosario—I have loved being in group with you. If anything, you have given me way more energy than the other way around. And I really mean that!

DAISY: [To Rosario] Do you believe him?

ROSARIO: Yes—actually I do. Thank you, Mark. And how about you, Mara? Have I driven you away?

MARA: Absolutely not, Rosario. I think you are awesome! I've enjoyed being with you and growing in here together.

ROSARIO: [To Daisy] Okay. I think I've had enough for now.

DAISY: Sure. But can you feel the sense of appreciation for you here?

ROSARIO: Yes, I really can!

DAISY: Okay. That's all I ask!

MARA: [To Rosario] Can you handle one more thing? Just something I'd like to share with you.

ROSARIO: Sure.

MARA: You know how you felt like a burden with your aunt and uncle after your mom died? Well, I felt not so much like a burden, but always like an outsider in my family. My mom and dad both remarried and both had two kids with their next spouses. I was the only child they had together, and they literally hated each other. So everybody had somebody on their team but me! So I really relate to how you feel, Rosario—I can really feel it, and I just really want you to hear that I feel very connected to you, and my leaving has only to do with me taking care of my own needs. You have been wonderful to be in group with, and I really want you to hear that from me!

ROSARIO: Okay, Mara. Thanks. I do. I will miss you.

MARA: Me too.

ROSARIO: So why are you leaving? No, don't answer that! You've already explained why and I get it. I just feel sad.

PETER: So, I'd like to encourage group members to feel into—in your body and in your emotions, what it is like to say goodbye. How is it to have really let each other in, to care and love, and to let go? How does that feel right now? For me, I feel a little like a piece of Velcro is being pulled off of my heart. It is hard to let go of Mara and Mark, but at the same time, I feel good about how you both are leaving.

RAJ: I feel good. I have seen many people come and go in my time, and I have gotten very philosophical about it. I want to wish you both all the best. You have enriched my life.

AMY: For me, I'm not philosophical like you guys. I feel a little abandoned and pissed at you guys for leaving, but I understand. I hope I'm not some kind of loser for sticking around.

RAJ: Hey—if you are a loser, what does that make me at 75 for being here?

AMY: I'm just saying how I feel, Raj! It's hard to be left behind. I'm an immigrant to this country. My family is thousands of miles away. It does not feel good to be left. I can tell you that!

RAJ: I too am an immigrant, Amy. I was just teasing you. I understand how you feel.

AMY: Okay. Thank you, Raj. It just hurts. It really hurts. I don't mean to blame you guys.

PETER: I'm glad you are sharing your feelings, Amy!

MARA: I feel really guilty now; I do not want you to feel abandoned, Amy!

AMY: Now I am pissed! Mara, I'm just sharing what is coming up for me. I'm not asking you to feel responsible for me! Can you understand the difference?

MARA: Yes, sure—I do get that, Amy. It can be hard for me not to take care of other people's feelings, but I hear that you don't need me to fix it.

AMY: I want you to take care of yourself—but I need to as well. You can't leave me and make me feel okay at the same time. You are just going to have to live with me wishing you weren't leaving and being a little pissed.

DAISY: Amy, I think in part you are saying how much Mara has meant to you.

AMY: Yes, and that I don't like her leaving, but I respect her choice.

MARA: For sure—I get that!

DAISY: We only have a few minutes left. Whatever you might want to say to Mark or Mara, now is the time.

SHARON: I'm really going to miss you, Mara. You have been great.

ROSARIO: I've had so many losses, and they came so early in my life. I've never had a chance to really talk about the feelings. It hurts, but it feels good at the same time to know I can handle it.

MARK: I've always hated goodbyes. I've always tried to avoid them. But I see the value in this. Saying goodbye this way I think will help me remember how much you guys have meant to me.

ROSARIO: I never had goodbyes. My experience has been that you wake up one morning and everybody is gone. So to tell you the truth, this has been a hard session, but I found out I can handle these feelings, and separate out a healthy goodbye from the kind of terrible abandonments that have happened in my past. That feels good.

Discussion

This particular group had stayed intact with stable membership for several years prior to the session recounted. This session demonstrates a group that has matured together, with group members who have grown to know each other quite well. A great many difficulties and conflicts had previously been sorted out and worked through. At an earlier, more formative phase of group development, differences and conflicts between members were messier and took more time to sort through. At this mature stage of group development, the group is able to work with differences quite readily by staying in good quality contact with each other, having prepared the ground for that over several years of work together.

Additionally, group members have created strong connections with each other. For instance, Raj and Amy have forged a strong connection around their immigrant experience. Mara and Rosario share the experience of being outsiders within their families of origin. Mara and Mark share the experience of having difficulty speaking up for themselves. As group members come to know each other at deeper levels and come to understand each other's life narratives, an unseen web forms that connects group members with each other. This web of connection supports a feeling of belonging for each group member which becomes an important support for integration and growth.

When we were writing this chapter on a sample GGT session, it just so happened that two members were leaving one of our groups, and so we wrote this up. Fortunately, though, the content of this session brings up some larger dimensions of GGT that we would like to briefly comment on in closing this chapter. All of life is impermanent. We are mortal, and even our most prized and precious relationships will one day end. At the same time, if we are to be alive emotionally, we must risk attachment and love even while we know that all relationships will end. In a sense, GGT is a microcosm of this existential reality. We come together in group, connect with each other, attach to each other, care for and even love one another. At the same time, we all know that the group will end and that the relationships formed are impermanent. In providing mutual support for taking the risks of attaching and loving while knowing that these and all relationships must end, GGT helps its members take the necessary risks of living and loving more fully.

Chapter 10

Charles Alexander

This chapter is written in Peter's voice

This chapter provides a discussion of the integration of individual gestalt therapy with GGT in long-term growth work. Although it is written in Peter's voice, both Peter and Daisy participated in the work with "Charles Alexander." Of course, the name and details have been changed to protect the client's anonymity. This chapter also includes a discussion of the application of three principles discussed in Chapter 1: presence, inclusion and clinical phenomenology. Our intention is to weave together the telling of Charles Alexander's story, how we worked with him, informed by gestalt therapy theory, and the changes that occurred for Charles in his way of living, his way of thinking, and how he approached his process of dying over the course of our work.

Charles Alexander was a business professor who came to me for psychotherapy in March, 1994. I worked with Charles intensively until his death from lymphoma in May, 2014. Charles and I worked together in both weekly individual psychotherapy and in a monthly day-long gestalt group that Daisy and I co-facilitated. Charles was 49 when we began our work and 69 when he died. Charles taught in a graduate school of business. His scholarship involved the study of business, political and military leaders, searching for those characteristics that lead to effective leadership. The relationship between leaders and the people working "under them" was fascinating to Charles. He experienced the world as profoundly hierarchical and competitive, and he explained to me that he had a reputation in the academic world for advocating a tough-minded, hierarchical approach to business leadership. Perhaps partly as a result of this worldview, Charles suffered tremendous anxiety about his own place in the hierarchical order within his family, at the university, and in his social life. In Charles's world, he was either at the top of the hierarchy, which felt exhilarating and necessary, or he was "on the outs," feeling deflated and terrible about himself. It was a strikingly binary experience of the world, with little room for compassion for himself or others.

In the first few individual sessions it became clear to me that Charles was suffering acutely. My notes from late 1994 reflect his complaints about having a terrible time finishing an important book he was writing with a colleague, serious health concerns as he had been recently diagnosed with lymphoma, a marriage that was in profound crisis due in part to Charles's multiple affairs, and a daughter with severe mental illness and substance abuse problems. A key factor in Charles's suffering was a tortured sense of self-loathing. He was intensely self-critical, with a retroflected contempt and self-hatred that was palpable and painful to sit with.

Along with the difficulties that caused Charles so much pain, he had many strengths. He was a New Englander (raised in New Hampshire) who had a wonderful, ironic sense of humor. He was highly intelligent, had a fabulous New England accent, was a handsome man, and was remarkably well spoken. Charles was highly literate. Interestingly, both Charles's greatest strength and greatest source of suffering lay in his relationships. He nurtured strong friendships and strong mentoring relationships, but also suffered agonizing fits of regret over mistakes he had made with people, over his parenting, and over having poisoned his marital relationship with many infidelities. While he had adversaries and competitors in the academic world, he also had colleagues to whom he was deeply loyal. He reported that there were many graduate students who were devoted to him, while others found him arrogant and off-putting. Charles did not suffer fools kindly. He could be sharp-tongued and dismissive with those he found wanting.

From the start Charles and I hit it off. I liked him very much, and I believe that he came to like me as well. You might even say that a certain measure of love developed between us, especially as we journeyed down the road of his dying process together.

After the first few sessions, I offered Charles an opportunity to try a topdog/underdog two-chair experiment around his experience of procrastinating on finishing a book he was working on with a colleague. This turned out to be very powerful for him, and became a touchstone that we would return to again and again. He was surprised at the force and contempt in his topdog, and even more surprised by the humiliation, shame, and fear of his underdog. This experiment offered him a safe space to cry, a release he had not allowed himself since childhood. This two-chair work also became a marvelous touchstone for us that came to represent the narcissistic split between Charles's grandiose aspect and his deflated aspect. This characterological polarity was present for Charles from the first day of our work to the last, but a great deal of healing occurred by the end, such that he could afford himself humor and compassion in these aspects as he grew emotionally.

Gestalt Group Therapy

I suggested that Charles consider joining a gestalt group that Daisy and I held twice a month in Berkeley. I explained that the group might be a useful adjunct to individual psychotherapy in that we could work with his issues in the interpersonal context of a group. Charles thought this was a good idea, and he participated in the gestalt group faithfully until his death 15 years later. That group would turn out to be an important source of support and an agent of change in Charles's life. Moreover, Charles deeply touched the lives of the other seven people in the group.

Our first group meeting occurred in April, 1997. It was a group of eight people—some straight, some gay—half were men and half women. All were professional people with a wide variety of personality styles. It so happened that this group was made up of a particularly high powered group of people, and in the first phases of the group they were quite competitive with each other. An incident occurred in the third month of the group that became a major touchstone for both the group and for Charles in our individual work. Charles talked in the group about how hurt he was about his wife's coldness toward him. He shed a tear. This was not a sob by any means; it was more of a "manly" tear down the cheek accompanied by a stoic expression. Matt, another group member, who, due to his stature as a forceful and imposing attorney, was probably at the top of the group hierarchy at that point, made the disparaging remark, "It's nothing to cry over!" While Charles wiped away the tear and chuckled in agreement with Matt's remark at the time, he was deeply wounded. We processed his hurt and anger at Matt in the following individual session.

A few weeks later, Charles was able to bring his hurt and anger over Matt's remark into the group. Our processing as a group of Matt's comment marked the beginning of the deepening of our group process. It began a process of opening up around issues of shame. It began a process of opening up around early trauma, and it began a process of intimate sharing. Matt was, for his part, taken aback by the hurt his comment had caused. He felt terrible about it, and it occasioned a softening in him that paved the way to his sharing about the physical abuse he suffered as a child at the hands of his mother, and how his competitive and insensitive father had frequently shamed him in childhood. This session had a powerful effect on all of the members of the group.

Over the course of time, something strange and unlikely occurred in the group. Three of the eight members were diagnosed with various forms of cancer. Charles was already fighting lymphoma, so now half the group was undergoing cancer treatments. I have no idea what the odds are of this occurring in a group of eight professional people, aged 40–60, but I imagine they are quite low. In any event, long odds or not, that is what happened. About 10 years into the group, Mary, a well-loved group member, who had become particularly close to Charles over the years, died suddenly of complications that arose in the treatment of her breast cancer. As the reader might imagine, her death hit the other group members very hard. Charles was deeply saddened by Mary's death.

Matt was also moved by Mary's death. Mary was an African American woman who had been a film-maker, and had completed a movie about the lives of incarcerated women just prior to her death. This movie was the culmination of Mary's life's work; she was passionate about film and issues of social justice. Matt had himself been diagnosed with melanoma about a year prior to Mary's death. Matt was inspired by Mary's completion of her film while fighting cancer, and decided to write a book about people who remain actively creative while coping with the challenges of living with cancer. Matt interviewed Charles for the book, and this interview became another source of friendship and camaraderie between them.

With the death of Mary, we now had three group members living with cancer, but Charles's condition was far more dire than that of the other group members living with the disease. The cancer had spread, and Charles was clear in his mind that eventually the disease would get the better of him.

Something that the group members found quite hilarious happened when we tried (and failed) months later to bring a new member in to replace Mary in the group. Daisy and I were hoping to have a new man join the group who happened to live in the same Silicon Valley college town as Charles. The new member's wife had been in graduate school at the university. As we told group members about this potential new member and gave his first name and profession, Charles asked one question after another about him. Finally he exclaimed, "No! We cannot bring him into the group! I know who this is and I've had an affair with his wife." Charles was at first mortified by this. After a stunned silence, all other members, men and women, gay and straight, broke into loud laughter and teased him, with many admiring comments about his virility. Soon Charles joined in the laughter, as his mortification melted into group hilarity. It was quite a moment, and for years afterward, and even after his death, the members in the group would share a laugh about it.

My Relationship with Charles

I have many favorite patients, but Charles was a favorite among favorites. He was conscientious—always there on time for both our weekly therapy sessions and for our twice-monthly group sessions. He worked hard—processing present-day and historical material with seriousness and a sense of purpose. We did not have a difficult relationship. There was not a lot of need for the repair of rupture between us. We had an excellent working alliance, and when issues did arise between us, we were able to work them through quite readily. I cannot recall a serious disagreement between us, yet I do not believe we were particularly confluent. We knew that we were different: me—a feeling, Jewish therapist type, and Charles—a flinty New England type. We were interested in each other—and quite aware of our differences. As a transference issue, I would say that Charles probably had something of an idealizing transference with me at first that evolved into more of a twinship transference, with strong feelings of friendship and brotherhood.

Sexual and Spiritual Issues

As our therapeutic relationship deepened, we were able to process sexual issues in the individual work that felt too vulnerable for Charles to work with in the group. He shared much about changes in his sexuality that occurred as he took chemotherapy drugs for the treatment of his cancer. The chemo had knocked out his libido. Concurrent with a decline in sexual interest, Charles took up mindfulness meditation at my encouragement. Charles had grown up in a strictly fundamentalist Protestant church and his mother was highly religious. Even as a child, Charles was not a believer. At church he felt equally bad publicly accepting its teachings (which made him feel like a hypocrite) or expressing his doubts (and feeling like an outcast and a soul bound for hell). Being a sexually charged adolescent, with normal adolescent male sexual curiosity and masturbatory behavior, Charles was terrified throughout childhood and adolescence that he was heading straight to hell upon his death and would spend eternity there. It will come as no surprise to the reader, therefore, that as an adult, he strongly embraced atheism. Charles's atheism was his refuge from an angry, demanding, anti-sexual god. Yet, as he grew emotionally and also as his sexual energy declined, the need to hide from a puritanical god also seemed to decline, and he opened up to a sense of the sacred in mindfulness meditation. I had recommended that Charles look into Jon Kabat-Zinn's mindfulness-based stress reduction. He found a local teacher, and became a regular meditator. Meditation gave Charles a new sense of centeredness and calm.

Charles's Sense of Self

At the beginning of our work, Charles's phenomenal world was marked by unremitting self-criticism, intense shame, and intense feelings of competitiveness, in which he was either the victor or the loser. Contempt was a strong theme in his relational world. When he was winning, he pointed the contempt outward at others; when he was losing, he pointed the contempt at himself. As I mentioned earlier, the topdog/underdog two-chair work, along with the crying incident in the group, had cracked these issues open, and over the course of 20 years of individual and group therapy, we did a great deal of work on Charles's grandiose and deflated aspects, and the contempt that kept those aspects so split off from each other. These issues arose again and again in his work, and represented the central fixed relational gestalts of his life. Contempt, narcissistic grandiosity and deflation, and difficulty with self-esteem regulation were very strong in him. They showed up intra-psychically, interpersonally, and relationally between us in our individual work.

Over time, Charles was able to cry with minimal shame, to express his care for me, to express his care for other members of the group, and to go a long way toward healing his relationship with his daughter. He became gentler and more patient as a parent. He hung in with his wife, who in some ways punished Charles until his death, and yet was a loyal and attentive caregiver. His capacity for loving relationships unquestionably increased, his sense of confidence improved, his self-hatred decreased, and he took more pleasure in his work. He worked with his expressions of contempt in intimate and work relationships, such that he learned to contain the contempt through awareness and mindfulness. This led to improvements in all of his relationships.

Charles's Academic Thinking

As Charles began to experience his life differently, his ideas about business leadership began to shift. Hierarchy, control, and competition no longer seemed the obvious state of affairs between people in business, and he began to write and teach about dimensions of leadership he had not considered before: cooperation, listening, and humility. He came to feel that competition was only part of the story. As he became more attuned to the growing role of empathy in his own life, he began to appreciate its importance in effective business leadership. He reported to me that his more current academic writing put a greater emphasis on empathy, cooperation, and altruism. He attributed this change in his thinking in part to our individual and group work.

An Issue Left Unspoken

By 2012 it was becoming increasingly clear that Charles's health was declining. The group members were very supportive, and, although it was painful (and triggering for the two other group members with cancer), the group stuck by Charles's side. Charles, who had been very sharp physically and mentally, was now frail and sometimes confused. At times he smelled mildly of urine when he came into the group room. The group members welcomed him with open arms.

A difficult issue arose as Charles was declining. He reported that his wife was becoming increasingly involved with another man, someone she had met at a business conference. Charles spoke rather elliptically about this, never directly accusing her of having an affair. It was obvious, however, from eye contact and facial expressions, that group members were distressed and mistrustful when Charles reported that his wife was on the computer and phone for hours with this man and flew to Seattle on multiple occasions to "work on a project" with him. At the same time, she took meticulous care of Charles—attending to his physical needs with a nurse's precision and always speaking with him in a calm, if cold, manner.

Leaving this issue unspoken—the obvious suspicion that she was having an affair and was probably preparing for a new relationship after Charles's death—was from my perspective an act of compassion on all of our parts. For Charles, his compromise solution with this issue seemed to involve equal parts of self-compassion, compassion for her, and denial. Or, to put it differently, there seemed to be an important creative adjustment at work in Charles's denial of something that would have been incredibly painful to contend with at such a vulnerable time in his life. Additionally for Charles, it was an act of compassion not to dwell on blaming her for this relationship. By this time Charles had taken full responsibility for the hurt he had caused her and damage he had done to his family with his own extramarital affairs. He said frequently that he treasured the rare moments of love and kindness that she shared with him, that he appreciated her caregiving, and he forgave her coldness, remembering that her coldness had settled in over years of his disregard for her feelings. He shared that while it was true that he had grown emotionally, he could not expect her to warm up to him just because he had changed. So no one in the group raised the question of whether she was having an affair. I believe it felt to us that this was one issue that was better left unspoken.

Our Last Individual and Group Sessions

It was now May 2014 and Charles was in hospice care. I went to visit him at his Silicon Valley home. Charles met me out front of the house and suggested that we walk. I was surprised that he had the energy and strength, but he kept a strong pace as we walked and talked. He told me that he still considered death to be the end, that he was not afraid of death itself, but fearful about a painful death. He expressed appreciation for the work we had done together, and we expressed our affection and care for each other. He seemed to be in an altered state, yet deeply connected to himself and to me. Startlingly, as we walked, he stepped out right in front of a moving car that had to slam on the brakes. I had an immediate adrenaline rush—and the driver glared angrily—but Charles took absolutely no notice. He just walked on and kept talking, looking back and motioning me onward! By the time we got back to the house, we had agreed that he would participate in one last group.

That last group ended up being at the hospital, as his condition had worsened prior to the scheduled group meeting. Charles had prepared a hospital meditation room for us. Charles greeted us and directed everyone as to where to sit in the circle of chairs he had set up. We had an extraordinary group meeting. We expressed our love for him, and he did the same for us. He said goodbye to each of us in turn, offering us each a little nugget of wisdom in what he had observed in our growth. In my career, that group meeting is something that will always stand out as a moment of great meaning and power.

Charles died three days later. The family held a private service and the university organized a memorial program. We did our own grieving in the gestalt group, with many tears, much laughter and many fond remembrances.

Understanding the Work from a Gestalt Therapy Perspective

Working with My Counter-transference

Dialogue lies at the heart of gestalt therapy. I was engaged in an ongoing dialogue with Charles from our first session until his death. Although the work was clearly focused on him, Charles had a profound impact on me.

There was, of course, much happening with me during the early work with Charles that I did not discuss with him—this was not my therapy; it was *his*. But for the purposes of this chapter, I will discuss some of the challenges I was facing in my personal life and what the work with Charles brought up for me, and look at what I chose to bring into our dialogue and what I chose to leave in the background.

I found Charles's self-loathing to be something I recognized in myself. My first marriage had ended some years prior, and my children were still young. The ending of that marriage was really the central crisis/trauma of my middle years. Leaving the marriage in hindsight looks like a strong decision, in that I, my children, and my former wife have thrived. But at the time, I was apprehensive about whether my children would thrive, and was prone to self-criticism. Therefore, Charles's self-loathing was more than a little triggering for me to encounter. Self-hate on the level that Charles was experiencing was a place I did not want to go, but at times the work with Charles could push me perilously close to those kinds of feelings.

Another factor that brought up my counter-transference with Charles was that his core issues triggered imagery, feelings, and memories of my father. My father had the combination of contempt, grandiosity, and self-hatred (a nasty narcissistic stew) that I felt present in Charles. In my father's case, his characterological issues got the better of him, and his life collapsed in his older years with severe depression and multiple psychiatric hospitalizations. So, I was triggered by Charles, but was working in my own therapy.

My personal therapy helped keep me from falling into the kind of despair and self-hate that Charles was mired in. Additionally, I was a member of a consultation group led by Stephen Johnson, the author of *Humanizing the Narcissistic Style* (1987). Johnson's profound understanding of the narcissistic style was a great support in the work with Charles, a case I frequently brought to the consultation group. With the supports of therapy and consultation, I was able to maintain a strong awareness of what was getting triggered, and I felt that, when I sat with Charles, I was quite available for dialogue with him.

Presence

All of the above was in the background for me when I sat with Charles in therapy—both the triggers and the supports. I tend to be a quite boundaried therapist, and I did not directly bring any of the issues described above into the therapeutic dialogue. Charles did not know about my prior divorce. He did not know about my father and the weight I carry related to my dad's struggles with narcissism. However, I think Charles sensed that I had an understanding of his struggles, even though he did not know the details of my life.

I have so far discussed what I *did not* bring into the dialogue: the details of my life. What I *did* bring was an emotional availability to Charles that was accessible for me and for him because I was working on my own issues and triggers. With strong sources of support for myself, the issues that Charles triggered in me helped me to empathize with his struggles. I often shared with Charles my here-and-now feelings that came up in relation to him and his work. For instance, when he was beating himself up for having been an impatient and neglectful father to his daughter, I often shared something about grieving, and frequently shared about my own grief—not tied to the content of my life, but specific enough to convey my personal experience. I did not make recordings of our sessions, but the following exchange would have been typical:

CHARLES: I wasn't there for my daughter. I would get so mad at her when she failed to act appropriately. I was so demeaning—just like my father was to me—yelling and so impatient. And now she is just a mess— on anti-psychotic medication—and just crazy as all hell. She's either gorked on the meds—which she hates and won't stay on—or just totally crazy. And really her mother tried, but I wasn't there for her.

PETER: I feel a lot of pain hearing you, Charles. I hear there is so much you regret. For my part, I feel that the issue really is embracing the grief and not turning it into self-hate. I find self-hate to be a destructive force in my life. I try to let myself grieve for my mistakes—having hurt or been insensitive to the people I love—but to be conscientious about not falling into self-hate.

CHARLES: I am working on that, but it is hard to forgive myself.

PETER: I can appreciate that. And I will do my best to hold that for you— the forgiveness. I happen to think that you have been a dedicated father—maybe not a perfect father, but a father who loves his daughter. And as I have said for some time, I think it is very possible, even probable, that your daughter's mental illness is primarily biological in nature, and not a result of your parenting.

CHARLES: Earlier in our work together I would have scoffed at this notion that you could hold out forgiveness for me, but now I feel differently, and it makes me feel good to have you do that.

PETER: It feels very good to me to have you accept this. I think that both you and I are getting better at sharing these more vulnerable feelings with each other. We're both learning how to welcome the gentler, more vulnerable, parts of ourselves.

CHARLES: I have always taken the vulnerable parts as weakness. I'm beginning to see the strength in vulnerability.

Charles and I had many sessions involving this kind of exchange. I share this in order to demonstrate one gestalt therapist's approach to presence; it involves walking a fine line in which I, as therapist, am very much involved but the work and the content are about the patient.

Inclusion

Inclusion in the dialogue with Charles came very readily to me—partly because I could relate to his character style and his turn of mind, and partly because I liked him. I enjoyed trying to put myself in his shoes in order to see the world from his perspective, and I appreciated the many ways in which Charles impacted me.

Charles was deeply engaged in trying to win back the trust and love of his wife. As I've said, she had turned to ice toward him during his many years of infidelity, and she would not or could not thaw. When she apparently became involved with another man, I worked to maintain a phenomenological attitude by appreciating Charles's perspective, and by bracketing off my own sense of outrage on his behalf. He was not well, I was feeling very protective of him, and I felt righteous indignation about my suspicion that his wife was taking up with another man at this time in Charles's life. Charles, at this point, knew that he would need her help as his cancer progressed, and he also had developed a remarkable empathy for her that included a compassionate sense of why she was so angry with him. As I mentioned earlier, Charles had evolved from a reactive atheism into a truly subtle sense of spirituality that, while not specifically Buddhist, was influenced by a Buddhist sensibility of mindfulness and compassion. He worked very earnestly at practicing mindfulness and compassion in his dealings with his wife. I endeavored to look at this situation from Charles's perspective. I saw little value in confronting his apathy or denial regarding her involvement with the man in Seattle. A typical exchange between us would have involved something like the following:

CHARLES: She is going to Seattle again to do more research with Sam. They seem to have gotten very close. I just wish she had some of those feelings for me—you know—wanting to be with me. She carries out her duties with me, but she always makes me feel like she'd rather be somewhere else.

PETER: I imagine it feels lonely to have her be this way with you. And I can imagine feeling pretty abandoned when she goes to Seattle to work with Sam.

CHARLES: Well, they are working on this project together and they spend a lot of time working on it. I wish she had the passion for me that she has for this project, but I think the work is good for her and this friendship is probably a relief from taking care of me.

This kind of exchange would unsettle me, in that Charles seemed to be willfully blind to her possible involvement with Sam, yet the willful blindness made perfect sense to me when I practiced listening to Charles with inclusion. His broad statements of compassion and empathy for her added a measure of wisdom to his way of looking at this, and I never went further than Charles in putting two and two together on this issue. It felt to me like the most compassionate approach. This approach was, I think, affirmed in its wisdom when I went with the group to see Charles at the hospital before his death. His wife met the group at the hospital, and it was clear that she was extremely attentive to him, and whatever complications existed in the marriage appeared to be superseded by their commitment to one another and to their family.

Clinical Phenomenology in Our Work

The work with Charles was phenomenologically grounded. Phenomenologically grounded gestalt therapy seeks to work with what is revealed by the client as the client experiences themselves in their life situation through the client's own experience and experiment, and not primarily via the therapist's interpretation of the experience. As I mentioned earlier, two powerful experiences that Charles had early on in our work were the two-chair exercise with the topdog encountering the underdog and Matt's shaming of Charles in the gestalt group around crying. Both of these were felt viscerally by Charles. New insights and awareness came to him by way of lived experience and struggle. They were deeply felt emotionally, somatically, and intellectually. They did not come by way of my interpretations; instead, they were supported by my dialogical attitude.

In the topdog/underdog work, Charles began to experience his topdog as the unforgiving/unrelenting taskmaster that had dominated his life. He connected this with his father, not through my interpretation, but through his own experience of the experiment with the two-chair work. Charles's underdog was terrified, and deeply ashamed. Charles felt this in his emotions, body, and mind. He connected this state with the shame he had felt as a child in his sexuality, his disbelief in Christianity, and the horribly deflated way he felt in reaction to his father's perfectionistic criticism. These insights and connections emerged spontaneously for Charles in the experience of the two-chair work, and provided the basis for years of dialogue between us.

The group work was also phenomenologically grounded, and Charles's experience of processing with Matt around Matt's shaming comment in reaction to Charles's tears was a courageous journey for Charles into staying with his experience and speaking his truth as he was experiencing it in the here and now of the group process. In the processing between Charles and Matt, Daisy and I saw our roles primarily as support for each of them to stay close to their experience, to speak their truth, and to stay in contact with themselves and each other. They both had powerful "Aha" experiences in this process. For the purposes of this discussion, I will stay with Charles's experience and will not describe Matt's except to say that this was a pivotal experience for him as well. As Charles encountered Matt, we encouraged Charles to attend to his somatic and sensory awareness, to bracket off his assumptions and projections about Matt, and to express in detail what he was feeling. He described feeling very angry and very embarrassed by what Matt had said. As he stayed with his experience, anger gave way to an "Aha" for Charles. He began to gain awareness of the hurt and wounded places in himself that Matt's comment had triggered. We encouraged Charles to stay with the emotional and somatic experience of being in the hurt and wounded place and to feel my support in his experiencing these feelings. This was a highly charged and cathartic experience for Charles with, at first, much anger and, later, many tears—and this time they were not controlled tears, but were deeply supported, fully embodied, letting-go crying. I must add that Matt joined in the crying, making the experience for Charles one of being joined rather than judged and shamed.

In both the two-chair work and the encounter with Matt, Charles had intense, cathartic experiences and began to gain awareness of the fact that his mode of creative adjustment was frequently shame-based and self-abusive. Of course, these intense experiences were the beginning of the growth process, not an end in themselves. Over years of careful, dialogically-based work together, Charles developed remarkable new capacities. Foremost among these was a new awareness of the awareness process itself. He became much better able to consciously self-regulate as he connected his self-loathing and contempt of others to his own history. His dedication to the awareness process opened him up to a non-religious, experientially-based practice of mindfulness. He learned how to be kinder to himself and others. This new awareness also helped him discover more in his academic work, making contributions in his field of business management that now emphasized cooperative and altruistic aspects of business leadership.

Conclusion

In our last individual meeting, when we walked around his Silicon Valley neighborhood, Charles asked about his impact on me. I shared with Charles that he had been an inspiration to me. The elements that could have dragged him or me into bitterness and despair—self-hate, contempt, and unconscious competitiveness—were issues that I had witnessed him struggle with, and had watched him make amazing progress with. I shared that his example inspired me and helped affirm for me that real change is possible. Charles shared with me that the therapy had opened up for him a new way of being and had helped transform his final 10 years into the best years of his life. He felt ready to face death, and felt essentially good about the life he had led.

I believe that the gestalt approach, based as it is on the phenomenological experience of the client, awareness and dialogue, proved an effective modality for working with Charles. I believe that if I had been primarily interpretive in our work, it may well have set up a problematic power dynamic between us. Being an academic and an independent, serious-minded thinker, Charles valued his own experience and took to the phenomenological method like a duck to water. He came to deeply cherish his awareness of his own process and way of being in the world. He felt a far greater sense of choice and agency in his life and gained in his capacity for gentleness, compassion, and love.

In the work of psychotherapy, we practitioners have the opportunity to touch many lives and to be touched by many. The process of psychotherapy is for the benefit of the patient, yet cannot help but change us as well. Charles touched my life in many ways. I thank Charles for his devotion to our work together, and for his extraordinary capacity for real change. I will always remember him and cherish his impact on my life.

Reference

Johnson, S. (1987). *Humanizing the narcissistic style*. New York: W.W. Norton.

Chapter 11

Social Awareness as a Dimension of Relational Development in Gestalt Group Therapy

This chapter is written in the voices of both Peter and Daisy

> *If we are to have peace, it is necessary to wage the peace. Otherwise, when their war comes, we also must hold ourselves responsible for it.*
>
> —Paul Goodman

In Chapter 2 we discussed nine aspects of relational development in GGT. In this chapter, we look at GGT members' relationship to the broader world, and consider *social awareness* as a vital component of relationality and relational development. We define social awareness thus: social awareness is comprised of several capacities:

- To think about one's social and political surround
- To feel one's connection with one's social and political surround
- To feel one's responses to occurrences in the broader social and political world
- To take empowered social action

Since we are always embedded in the broader field, feeling one's connection with the social and political surround is fundamental to responsive, responsible, and empowered living. GGT seeks to support the development of group members' social awareness primarily by creating an inclusive, democratic, and supportive group culture. The group becomes a facilitative environment for social responsiveness not by the promotion of any political ideology, but by supporting the group members' experience of their connection with, and responses to, the broader field. In this exploration, we will be guided primarily by the work of three of gestalt therapy's leading social thinkers: Philip Lichtenberg, Paul Goodman, and Erv Polster.

Dr. Philip Lichtenberg is a gestalt therapist with whom I (Peter) had the good fortune to study at the Bryn Mawr College Graduate School of Social Work and Social Research. Lichtenberg explicates a "liberation psychology" (1990), in which all members of society are deeply shaped by abusive, competitive, and divisive forces in the modern social order, and the work of social change necessarily includes addressing the effects of these. In his work, Lichtenberg brings to bear clinical insights from socially progressive psychoanalytic and gestalt therapy voices, including those of Sigmund Freud, Alfred Adler, Sandor Ferenczi, Paul Goodman, Erv Polster, and others. Although Freud is usually thought of as a pessimistic, conservative thinker, Lichtenberg argues that, within Freud's writings, there are two distinct and often contradictory threads: the radical Freud who espouses self–social unity, and the conservative Freud who espouses self–social disparity. Lichtenberg's work provides an invaluable theoretical framework for understanding how GGT can support its participants in developing their social awareness.

Dr. Paul Goodman, as a co-author of gestalt therapy's founding book, *Gestalt Therapy: Excitement and Growth in the Human Personality* (1951), helped set gestalt therapy's orientation to the social dimensions of health. Quite distinct from a psychotherapy that seeks to help the client adjust to the modern impersonal age, Goodman sought, in developing gestalt therapy, an approach that would honor the self-regulation of individual, group, and community (Stoehr, 2013). With gestalt therapy, he developed a deeply humanistic approach in which people and groups could self-regulate according to their needs, aspirations, and desires. He was inspired by Jeffersonian republican ideals of a decentralized, democratic social order. He was suspicious of bureaucratic power, including that of corporate power, and governments of the left, right, or center. As his biographer, Taylor Stoehr (2013, pp. 16–17), says:

> For the therapist living in the age of the organized system this meant attempting to revivify face-to-face community and to reclaim traditional values, endeavors that were moral and political as much as they were physicianly or pastoral. Goodman's conception of therapy began with the awareness that healing could not occur in isolation from culture and, further, that in our times culture itself was in need of healing.

Dr. Jack Aylward, in his outstanding book on the social dimensions of gestalt therapy, *Gestalt and the American Experience* (2012, pp. 180–181), discusses the seamlessness and complementarity between Fritz Perls's therapeutic innovations and Paul Goodman's commitment to social change:

> What Fritz tackled in the therapeutic setting Goodman wrestled with, more generally, in his activist participation throughout a wide range of social, political, and artistic concerns, continually striving for the types of changes he believed were at least as critical as individual therapy for the well being of his patients. The focused work of Fritz's clinical genius and Paul's humanistic worldview incorporated

what both believed to be those necessary and sufficient conditions that supported overall therapeutic vitality. By using this more inclusive lens, we can begin to appreciate those confluent connections that occur between what we as therapists do clinically and the relevancy of all of that with respect to a variety of environmental concerns.

While Goodman shows us the unity of psychotherapy, culture, and society, Dr. Erving Polster (2015) fleshes out the relationship between psychotherapy and community from a somewhat different vantage point, and establishes the creation of new community-based large groups that borrow from psychotherapy's insights. He names these large groups "Life Focus Communities." Polster is gestalt therapy's gentle radical who takes no commonly held assumptions for granted. One of those assumptions is the separation between psychotherapy and community life. Another of those assumptions is the separation between the secular psychotherapeutic perspectives and traditional religious perspectives. Polster bridges these separate worlds in his establishment of Life Focus Communities that bring to everyday people, in community-based settings, the best of traditional community life along with the affirmation and guidance provided by religious life (without resort to the supernatural), all informed by psychology's insights into the human condition and psychotherapy's roadmaps for growth and healing. Polster's Life Focus Communities have much in common with GGT in their focus on "the powers of communal togetherness and its paradoxical advocacy of individual freedom" (Polster, 2006, p. 168). We have found that such an atmosphere provides excellent soil for the emergence of greater and more refined social awareness among group members.

In this chapter we will speak of a person's "social surround." Let us take a moment to define that term. In referencing a person's social surround we are thinking of that which tends to come to the foreground when a person thinks of her society. It is a subjective experience that we are referring to since there are myriad ways in which one could place a person in her society from the outside. A person's social surround is the society that she experiences living in. A person's social surround is not fixed and shifts in different contexts. In this chapter we will discuss several group members, all of whom managed to create greater social awareness through their involvement with GGT. For one person, his social surround is the church that failed to protect him from childhood sexual abuse. For another group member, her social surround is the experience of being a black woman in a world filled with white women who take the privilege of their whiteness for granted. For another, the social surround consists of being a Jewish person with intergenerational family trauma, dealing with the ascendancy of Donald Trump and white nationalism. For another, the social surround is the discomfort that comes from having been an insider in an elite world, but having been excluded because of her gender identity.

We also use the term "support" liberally in this chapter, and would like to share a definition of support from Philip Lichtenberg (1990, p. 142):

> *I define support as any element or collection of elements, internal or external, that makes for the ability to proceed with a sense of integrity through an experience that is novel. That which preserves and encourages a person's felt integrity in the presence of new and thus challenging conditions can be taken as support to that person.*

We appreciate Lichtenberg's definition and find it relevant to this chapter on social awareness, because we have found that the development of social awareness requires exactly the kind of support he is describing: holding a group member with respect and connection while they explore deep-seated and difficult social experiences.

Principles for Developing Social Awareness in Gestalt Group Therapy

Drawing on Lichtenberg's liberation psychology, Goodman's writings on community, and Polster's work on Life Focus Communities, we have developed a few principles for the development of social awareness in GGT. In this chapter we will explain and explore each of these principles and how they apply in GGT, interspersed with some relevant case material. Below, we list four principles that guide our approach to promoting social awareness in GGT:

1. We seek a sense of community and connectedness, wherein GGT members may derive mutual support for thinking and feeling in new ways in relation to their social surround.
2. We seek human contact and dialogue among equals.
3. In a psychology of self–social unity, the individual's experience of acting on their emotions will tend to enhance the well-being of society.
4. We seek to support group members' differentiated responses to the field: their emotional response, subjectivity, autonomy, and agency in relation to their social surround.

We Seek a Sense of Community and Connectedness, Wherein GGT Members May Derive Mutual Support for Thinking and Feeling in New Ways in Relation to Their Social Surround

In recent years, Erv Polster has turned his considerable intellect and imagination to the development of Life Focus Communities, an innovative approach to creating large groups that support a deeply humanistic approach to living well and fully. We consider Polster's Life Focus Communities to be closely related to GGT. Polster (2015, p. 193) refers to Life Focus Communities as psychotherapy's "social offspring." We think of his Life Focus Communities as GGT's first cousin. Both Life Focus Communities and GGT provide new and different ground for the group member to stand on. This ground is different from the group member's usual family and social milieu. It is a place of support and connection from which the group member may gain new perspectives on his life. In so doing, the group member may develop a stronger, more aware connection to his social surround.

Life Focus Communities are different from GGT in that they are not a form of psychotherapy; instead, Life Focus Communities borrow from many of psychotherapy's insights and methodologies for the purpose of fostering awareness, community, and a sense of meaning in their participants. What Life Focus Communities *do* have in common with GGT is that both are engaged in bringing people together, fostering community, and developing within that community a sense of connectedness. A vital dimension of that connectedness is the connection to our social surround. In Polster's words: "The mission I am describing for the Life Focus Community is broader than that of private therapy, and it is explicitly designed to go beyond attention to troubled lives into examining how people at large live with each other" (p. 165). Ultimately, the group member's connection to his social surround may awaken a sense of responsibility for participating in social change.

Connectedness to one's social surround begins with awareness. This awareness can be particularly difficult to support when one's relationship to one's social surround is fraught with strong emotions such as fear and anger. In addition to strong emotions, there are often fixed gestalts involved in this arena: complex patterns of identification and alienation that come into play when group members begin to unpack and gain awareness of their relationship with their social surround. Group members frequently develop awareness of deeply embedded patterns of adaptation to their social surround when given the stimulation and support of gestalt group therapy. Commonly, we see awareness start with personal childhood experiences, and subsequently extend out to the broader social surround.

Working through a Fixed Gestalt: Identification with the Abuser

Matt is a straight, white, 52-year-old lawyer. He never knew his father, and his mother worked as a waitress. Matt was raised Catholic, and his very religious mother was involved in the neighborhood parish. As was all too common in his childhood era, Matt's parish priest started molesting him when Matt was very young. The abuse continued throughout Matt's childhood. Matt grew up to be a very conservative, anti-abortion, anti-gay Catholic. He started therapy when his wife threatened to leave him due to his depression and problem drinking.

In individual therapy, Matt began to talk for the first time about his childhood abuse. He also soon came to see that he had a problem with alcohol, and at first reluctantly, and later enthusiastically, participated in Alcoholics Anonymous (AA). After a year of individual therapy and AA, Matt joined an ongoing gestalt therapy group co-facilitated by Daisy and Peter. It was here, with group support, that he began to gain awareness of a fixed gestalt that had been powerfully shaping his perceptions up to this point in his life: identification with the priest who had molested him and the church who had protected that priest.

Matt had held the conviction that he was himself primarily responsible for the abuse, and said in group: "These things happen all the time with curious teenagers." He harbored no ill will toward his offending priest, who "was a good priest." In sharing his story with the group, Matt was met with much empathy, but also outrage at how he had been victimized. One group member asked for clarification: "Didn't you tell us that the abuse started when you were a little kid, not when you were a teen? How can you blame it on your teenage sexual curiosity?" This comment, along with much group support, opened up in Matt a whole new arena of feeling and responses. Group members asked Matt new and novel questions, such as "Why didn't the church protect you?" As Matt looked into this question, his research both shocked him and sounded all too familiar. He found an old newspaper account of several local priests being sent to Matt's community from other states precisely because of accusations of molestation in those places. Matt became convinced that his offending priest was one of those who had been shuffled away from a distant community, only to offend in his community—against him!

Over time, Matt became much more aware of his process of identifying with his abuser, and came to see that it was the priest who was responsible for the molestation and not himself. This deepening awareness catalyzed a dramatic change in Matt's worldview.

Matt was now was able to see and feel his own life and circumstances from his own vantage point, greatly enhancing the quality in GGT we know as "presence." New presence and aliveness infused his intellectual and relational life. He left his conservative Catholic congregation, and found a new, social justice-oriented Catholic community. He wrote a moving story of his abuse which he published in a progressive Catholic journal. Along with a sense of connection to his own story, Matt also found sobriety with the support of his AA involvement, and largely overcame a depression that had primarily been the result of a great deal of retroflected anger at his abuser and the institutions that supported that man.

We share Matt's story here because it illustrates the significance of the gestalt group as a mutually supportive community in which group members can discover a different center of gravity than their usual family and social milieu. Ensconced as Matt was in his conservative, hierarchical church and his religious family, before his involvement in GGT he did not have the separateness required to think and feel differently about his abuse. With the support of individual therapy, GGT, and AA, all of which provided new ground for him to stand on, Matt was able to work through the fixed gestalt of identification with his abuser, and to develop new energy for and understanding of his social surround.

We Seek Human Contact and Dialogue among Equals

In this increasingly impersonal and technologically-driven world, GGT stands resolute in its low tech, physical, humanness. The power of simply forming a circle in a room with other people and being with them cannot be underestimated. In recent decades, the basic skills required for citizenship have diminished. These include the ability to be with and converse with others, and the ability to discuss with others the conditions of our lives. Paul Goodman (2011, p. 43) writes that "group psychotherapy is identical with contactful neighbor-love that pays attention and comes across." We appreciate Goodman's image of the group as connection between neighbors in that neighbors are fellow citizens of the larger field that encompasses neighborhood, country, and world. Goodman was a great proponent of informed and responsible citizenship that can stand sensibly against injustice, impersonal bureaucracy, inequality, and violence. GGT lays the groundwork for the process of promoting such citizenship simply by creating a space for members to be in a room together for the purpose of making contact with each other.

In GGT, all group members, including the leader, meet as equals, providing mutual support for many aspects of growth, including their developing social awareness. Although the leader certainly has a unique role to play in the group, has different responsibilities than group members, and must maintain professional boundaries within the group, she too meets as an equal. No less than other group members, the leader is impacted by her society, and bringing the sensibility of herself as a social agent is important. The leader must be careful not to privilege certain opinions or she might lose her ability to act as a facilitator for each group member's exploration of their social experience. Her role here requires skill and subtlety. She balances joining with the group in their explorations of their social experiences, being clear that she too is impacted by conditions in the larger field, while maintaining her role as the facilitator of all group members' explorations, and not privileging her view or that of any group member.

Developing greater social awareness is everyone's business. GGT does not cast some group members as oppressors and others as oppressed; instead, we see all group members (and all members of society) as in some ways participating in, and in other ways resisting, unjust and oppressive aspects of the current social order. As Lichtenberg (1990) points out, we have all made, psychologically and socially, powerful adaptations to the society in which we live regardless of our position or rank in that society. Thus we are all, in various ways, invested in the status quo. Those who are perceived to be powerful and those who are perceived to be powerless are equally respected in GGT. Discussions of anti-Semitism equally involve Jewish and non-Jewish members. Discussions of racism equally include members of all colors. Discussions of money and class equally include rich, poor, and middle-class group members. All group members are supported in expressing themselves, listening to each other, and learning from each other's perspectives. Such discussions inevitably bring forth differences that become opportunities for contact and dialogue among group members.

Welcoming all the Voices of the Field

Our group was about mid-session. Our one male member was out for the day due to a recent surgery, and in attendance were nine white women and one African American woman. Several of the white women discussed and worked on a variety of issues in the group. At one point, Lynne, the African American woman, became quite upset and shared with much agitation, "I have an issue with white women. I just want to say to all of you white women here 'you have been handed the world, and all you do is complain!' "

Our orientation is to give support for the many narratives that form in GGT, and we felt it very important to give Lynne support in voicing her feelings. We asked her to say more. "If I don't speak up, I will have to leave the group." I [Peter] assured her that her feelings were welcome just as all members' feelings are welcome. "I find it really hard with white women. I do much better with men, and I really miss Bill" (Bill, the member who was out, happens also to be white) "because he is also different from the rest of you, and I don't feel like as much of an outsider when he is around."

One of the white women, Gladys, said, "I am very open to your feelings, but I also want to feel safe bringing up what's happening in my life."

LYNNE: I just need to share what I'm feeling—because if I didn't, I would have to leave the group. I feel like I'm breaking some kind of rule here by speaking up like this!

GLADYS: Yes, I get that! I feel like I'm breaking the rules too—like I'm doing something wrong.

PETER: I just want to step back, and say to the whole group that each person's perspective is valued here. Talking about issues of race is never easy, and since our society is in such turmoil around these issues, we are necessarily going to feel difficulty and discomfort in here when we bring race into the group process. The main thing I want to say to everyone in the group is that this discussion is important. We all need space to talk about race, and we are not going to do it right. We might step on each other's toes with this discussion, but as long as the other person can say "ouch," then we can work our way through just about any difficulty.

LYNNE: I want to bring all of me to this group. And part of that is my anger, but also part of that is my love. So as long as I can bring it all in, then I am okay.

GLADYS: And is it okay with you when I talk about my issues?

LYNNE: As long as it is okay with you that I can bring in my reactions.

GLADYS: Yes, of course.

LYNNE: Then I am okay.

GLADYS: Me too.

Of course this dialogue went on with much more sharing from Gladys, Lynne, and other group members. We bring up this vignette to illustrate the concept of meeting as equals. The narrative of each group member is respected and seen as adding to group wisdom. If the group silences a person of color or any group member who is part of a minority group, then that person is being forced to fuse with the group's dominant narrative. On the other hand, if the leader gives "official sanction" to the perspective of a group member who may be seen as disadvantaged, then the leader is setting up a new power structure in the group, inhibiting dialogue, and creating a new master narrative. In GGT, all "master narratives" are antithetical to the principles of equality and dialogue. Our task is to facilitate dialogue among *equals*. If everyone's voice is heard and respected, then we learn that those who appear to have all of the privilege are themselves deeply constrained and those who appear to have no privilege exercise their power in a variety of ways. Our lives all contain a complex mix of privilege and oppression.

Dialogue has a way of uncovering the complexities of power and privilege in all of our lives. Lichtenberg's liberation psychology helps us understand that an experience of unhealthy dominance and constricting fusion takes place when either Lynne has no authority to speak to her experience of anger at the white women in the group or Gladys becomes intimidated by Lynne's expression of her feelings as a black woman and suppresses her own experience. This is the fusion of dominance: one person's narrative becomes the dominant "master narrative" and all other group members must fuse to that narrative. Meeting as equals in GGT means that all perspectives are honored and the work of the group is found in the dialogues that unfold as we speak to our own perspective while also hearing each other's perspectives.

Dialogue, then, is the soil from which social awareness springs, for in expressing ourselves and hearing each other, we differentiate from the fusions of dominance and connect more deeply with our own experience and responses. As we will explore in the next section, this grounding in our experiences and responses often brings forth a new sense of responsibility for participating in the social surround: it is the voice of social awareness.

In a Psychology of Self–social Unity, the Individual's Experience of Acting on Their Emotions Will Tend to Enhance the Well-being of Society

As we discussed in Chapter 1, GGT takes an approach of self–social unity as opposed to self–social disparity in its view of working with the connection between affect and action. In my (Peter) 1998 article, "Affective Process in Gestalt Therapy," I presented a model that views affect as the organism's response to the field, which with support and awareness points toward empowered action. In GGT's psychology of self–social unity (Lichtenberg, 1978), our emotional responses are a form of intelligence that, when we are given sufficient support for *awareness*, point us to empowered, effective action. On the other hand, when the emotions are at play outside of awareness, they will tend to get acted out with less effectiveness and less integration. Sometimes, outside of awareness, emotions will get acted out destructively.

Since we are always embedded in the larger field, which includes our community, society, country and world, the emotions we feel relate to all that we are a part of. At times, a person's emotions point to action they might take in their intimate relationships. With further awareness, those same emotions may inform social action.

Two Examples of Emotions Informing Action

Jane's younger brother is disabled and in a wheelchair. He frequently needs Jane to transport him to the doctor, do shopping, etc. However, he never directly asks for Jane's help, assuming instead that it is simply Jane's job to take care of him. Moreover, Jane's brother is frequently obnoxious and rude to Jane when Jane does help. In group, Jane is feeling a great deal of anger about this situation. We "put her brother in the empty chair" and Jane expresses her anger at the imagined person sitting there. In this piece of work, Jane discovers how responsible she was made to feel as a child for her younger brother's disability. With this new awareness of the meaning of her anger, Jane reports in the next session that she set a limit with her brother for the first time in her life. She let the brother know that, from now on, if he wants her help, he will have to ask for it politely and not be abusive to her.

The emotions a person feels may be related to broader, societal issues, and with support, the feelings may point the person in the direction of social action.

With the group's support, Jane makes better contact with her anger. At one level, the anger is a *signal* that she needs to assert herself with her brother and that it is not okay for him to take her for granted and to treat her disrespectfully. At a deeper level, the anger is a *symbol* that points toward a broader social awareness for Jane. At this level, her feelings are simmering and strong—they reach toward the broader field. Over time and with much dialogue among group members, Jane becomes aware of the sexism in her family of origin. She, as the only sister, was designated by her parents to be her brother's caregiver. Her two other brothers did little of the caregiving for her disabled brother. It all fell to Jane. Since Jane's mother was alcoholic and subject to abuse from her father, Jane was held in a highly abusive, exploitive family system, that was itself part and parcel of a sexist society that supported this kind of differential treatment of girls within families.

Jane's social awareness grew over many years of her involvement with the group, and her political/social awakening had a profound impact on her life choices. She found that she no longer was willing to be in a monogamous, heterosexual relationship in which many of the patterns of her childhood were being repeated. She opened up in her sexual relationships, finding that she was more fulfilled being bisexual and polyamorous than she had been in monogamy. She also got involved with women's music, and joined a women's drumming circle. Now she was much more lively, fun, and funny in group. She

had worked her way through retroflected anger to a life of more freedom, self-expression, and social awareness.

In another case in point, Sarah's work with the group around her fear
helped transform the fear into anger, excitement, and social action.

> Following the election of Donald Trump, Sarah is talking in group
> about her feelings of fear. Her grandparents were holocaust survi-
> vors who rarely talked about their experiences, but passed on intense
> feelings of shame and fear to Sarah's mother, who in turn was fre-
> quently depressed and neglectful of Sarah and her sister in childhood.
> Sarah, who is single, has been avoiding people since the election, and
> has been going home, smoking marijuana, watching TV, and isolat-
> ing after work. The social trauma experienced by many after the
> Trump election resonated through her personal trauma, and she felt
> immobilized.
>   With much support from the group, Sarah talked about her fear,
> her immobilization, her family history, and her isolating. Although
> talking through all of this was difficult and painful for Sarah, with
> group support she was able to get underneath the immobilization,
> and start to feel some excitement and energy. One group member
> told Sarah that the existentialist writer, Albert Camus, once said that
> he never in his life felt so alive as when he was fighting in the French
> resistance. With group support, Sarah, like Camus before her, began
> to feel more alive. With increased awareness of the many layers of
> trauma that the Trump ascendancy had triggered in her, Sarah began
> to feel more empowered, and the fear started to be replaced by anger.
> The anger fueled Sarah to take action, and she decided to volunteer
> at a local Planned Parenthood office, giving support and guidance to
> vulnerable teen girls.

These two cases illustrate GGT's field theory and its approach of self–
social unity. We view affect as a kind of intelligence that informs us of our
responses to the field. With support, our feelings can act as signals that
help shape our awareness of the field and guide effective action. Our feelings can also symbolize our response to conditions in the greater social
surround and fuel social action that will be both satisfying to engage in
and a benefit to our world.

We Seek to Support Group Members' Differentiated Responses to the Field: Their Emotional Response, Subjectivity, Autonomy, and Agency in Relation to Their Social Surround

Group members are always a part of their social surround—the broader
society of which they are a part. Making contact with the social surround

is like making contact with any aspect of our experience: it requires both connection and autonomy. Both ends of this contact polarity—connection and autonomy—require support.

Paula is a trans-sexual psychiatrist in her mid-forties, who is now a woman but was born a boy. She grew up in an upper-class family in Greenwich, Connecticut. Her father was a wealthy Wall Street man. Paula attended an Ivy League school and served as vice-president of the Young Republicans there as a young man. She knows many people who are ensconced in positions of power and feels very connected to government and business elites. Yet, since coming out, her powerful family has been abusive and rejecting of her. Her sense of *connection* to the society she was bred to be an elite member of is now extremely complicated. She goes back and forth between, on the one hand, feeling connected with her peers and, on the other hand, feeling completely alienated from them. Her sense of connection with her social surround is filled with conflict, and attending to the many feelings that come up in relation to it requires a great deal of group support.

Paula's sense of *autonomy* from her social surround is also quite complicated. While she does feel separate from her social surround, hers is generally not an empowered sense of separateness. Her separateness from her family and peers feels to Paula more like rejection than empowered autonomy. She therefore requires a good deal of support in feeling a greater sense of her locus of control as lying within her own center. In GGT, Paula has worked, with much group support, on developing healthier boundaries and not introjecting the disdain with which her family and many friends have treated her since coming out.

Paula has said in group, "Being trans is a very radicalizing experience." In working through many aspects of her connection to and autonomy from her family and peers, Paula has found herself with a changing and deepening social awareness. Although at one time a committed conservative Republican, Paula now sees herself as a "liberal libertarian"—someone who cherishes civil liberties and gives generously to the American Civil Liberties Union and the Southern Poverty Law Center. She has reflected on the confluent power of growing up in the arms of wealth and status. Gaining distance from her identification with the powerful has opened up a new sense of humanity and compassion in Paula.

It is never easy to differentiate oneself from one's social surround in the service of developing greater social awareness. GGT can support this process by staying connected with group members and supporting their integrity as they do the hard, and sometimes disorienting, work of searching for their own truth—truth which may challenge a person's deeply held identifications, attitudes, and positions that have been shaped over a lifetime of creatively adjusting to oppression and injustice in our world.

We would like to close this chapter with a quotation from Paul Goodman (2011, p. 43): "We must see that many acts commonly regarded as legal and even meritorious are treason against our natural society, if they involve us in situations where we cease to have personal responsibility and concern for the consequences." Here, Goodman is calling for an end to confluence with a society where injustice, violence, racism, homophobia, war, and ecological decline are normalized. At its best, GGT provides the "natural society" that Goodman is describing, along with many of the benefits of Polster's Life Focus Communities, where group members' connection with each other brings them to new awareness and contact with their social surround. This new awareness and contact can catalyze group members to take greater responsibility for their part in their society. It is at the junction where new awareness begets new contact and new action that GGT can support group members in becoming agents of social change.

References

Aylward, J. (2012). *Gestalt therapy and the American experience.* Queensland, Australia: Ravenwood Press.

Cole, P. (1998). Affective process in psychotherapy: A gestalt therapist's view. *Gestalt Journal, 21*(1), 49–72.

Goodman, P. (2011). *The Paul Goodman reader.* Oakland, CA: PM Press.

Lichtenberg, P. (1978). *Lectures in psychoanalysis for social workers.* West Hartford, CT: University of Connecticut School of Social Work.

Lichtenberg, P. (1990). *Community and confluence: Undoing the clinch of oppression.* New York: Peter Lang.

Polster, E. (2006). *Uncommon ground: Harmonizing psychotherapy and community to enhance everyday living.* Phoenix, AZ: Zeig, Tucker & Theisen.

Polster, E. (2015). *Beyond therapy: Igniting life focus community movements.* Piscataway, NJ: Transaction Publishers.

Rich, A. (1971). The Blue Ghazals. In *The Will to Change.* New York: W.W. Norton.

Stoehr, T. (2013). *Here now next: Paul Goodman and the origins of gestalt therapy.* New York: Taylor & Francis.

Chapter 12

The Journey

This chapter was written in the voices of both Peter and Daisy

The heroic struggle today is to explore and map anew the human spirit and the nature of human interaction.
—Miriam Polster

In making something whole, I discover my wholeness.
—Joseph Zinker

Theory as a Road Map on the Journey

One of our guiding images in gestalt group therapy is that of the caravan. Group members and leaders are on a journey of growth, integration, self-acceptance, individuation, empathy, connection, and empowerment. We find in GGT that the hero/heroine's journey is best undertaken with plenty of support and connection—we all need a caravan to travel with, lest we each are exposed to the elements alone in the desert.

The journey to aliveness, engagement in the world, risk-taking, and connectedness is the grandest journey of all. And like all archetypal journeys, it can be terrifying at times. It involves contending with each other in group, grappling with our demons, being lost, getting found, experiencing rupture and repair. We need each other to do this work, which is hallowed by the group that confronts us, challenges us, cries with us, laughs with us, calls us to account, and, most importantly, belongs to us: passionately counting us as one of its members, and refusing to give up on us, even when we have shown the parts of ourselves of which we are the most ashamed.

We have found that gestalt group therapy provides a model that is strong enough to hold these kinds of group together, and we hope this book has been a useful bridge to GGT both for gestalt therapists who conduct groups in a more traditional gestalt format and for group therapists who work from other theoretical frameworks. For gestalt therapists, we have hoped to provide theory and methodology as a bridge to working more fully with an interactive group process. Without theory and methodology, the interactive modality can feel chaotic. Therefore, we have sought to organize and map out a sound intellectual framework so that gestalt therapists will have access to underlying structures and emergent processes that can bring beauty and order to the interactive group process. We hope to have introduced group therapists practicing from other theoretical frameworks to gestalt therapy's unique history, methodology, theory, and flavor.

Sound theory is the foundation for effective practice. Particularly when sand storms temporarily blind the GGT leader and threaten to throw the whole caravan off course, theory is the GGT practitioner's reliable map and compass. Throughout this book, we have endeavored to provide sound, reliable theory to help practitioners with some of GGT's most daunting challenges and greatest opportunities.

GGT Leadership as a Vocation

Throughout the many discussions in this book, we have been focused on the growth and life of the client. But what of the therapist? Group leadership offers many, often daunting, challenges for the leader. When the leader works with these challenges consciously, the gestalt group can be as rich and rewarding for the leader as it is for the group members. There are few experiences more exciting for a group leader than recognizing the distance a member has traveled on their journey to aliveness. The group leader herself travels a parallel path of growth. From the day she first sits in the leader's chair she is confronted by tests of her skill and of her own character. Can she maintain her balance in the face of the many feelings directed at her and other group members? Can she sustain an open heart when members show their least likable aspects? Can she allow her vulnerability and humanity to be manifest in the group? All of these challenges take on meaning as we become increasingly aware of the powerful impact gestalt group leadership has on our personal and professional development.

The path of GGT leadership has taught us to be tender and forgiving in the face of the many foibles we must face in ourselves and in our group members. It has taught us to be resilient when we feel that we are on the right path, but are facing opposition from the group. It has taught us to speak our truth when we feel that it is important to do so. GGT leadership has taught us that we must continually be open to learning about our own shadow sides. It has taught us to value the healing properties of forgiveness, humor, and gentleness. It has taught us that social awareness and social engagement are integral aspects of health—for healthy people cannot exist outside of healthy, diverse communities embedded in healthy, diverse, ecosystems.

The path of GGT leadership has provided us with opportunities to help create community. It has helped us to appreciate that a sacred space can be fostered when people come together with the intention of listening to and supporting one another. It has helped us appreciate that each person's life is complex, mysterious, and deeply connected to the greater whole. These lessons have shaped not just our work but also ourselves as human beings, and for that we are grateful.

References

Polster, M. F. (1992). *Eve's daughters: The forbidden heroism of women* (p. 180). San Francisco, CA: Jossey-Bass.

Zinker, J. (1977). *Creative process in gestalt therapy* (p. 239). New York: Random House.

Afterword

Resistance and Survival with Gestalt Group Therapy

This afterword is written in the voices of both Peter and Daisy

We are writing this short afterword in the week following the 2016 U.S. election. As of this writing, the new president has not taken office, but humanists everywhere, both in the US and outside of it, are concerned about what the future might hold. We feel that the next four years will be a serious time in which thinking people in general, and gestalt group therapists in particular, will face new difficulties and challenges. In this afterword we will discuss our concerns for the future, the impact of oppression on gestalt groups, and some reasons for hope.

Our Concerns

As we sit here, a week after the election, our concerns are numerous. In particular, we would like to consider the impact on ourselves and our clients when leaders potentially suffer from serious character disorders. Although it is not possible to diagnose a person from afar, in the current situation, we think it prudent to consider Dr Otto Kernberg's concept of malignant narcissism. According to Kernberg, "When intense pathology of aggression dominates in a narcissistic personality structure, the pathological grandiose self may become infiltrated by egosyntonic aggression, antisocial behavior, and paranoid tendencies, which translate into the syndrome of malignant narcissism" (2004, p. 20). This condition does not improve or resolve with the acquisition of power. Instead, its attendant paranoia is only exacerbated by the fact that the illusion that pain can be relieved through aggrandizement has now been shattered. Now, there is nothing to do but to objectify and blame "the other" with increasing rage and ferocity. When a person with malignant narcissism acquires great political power, we see little possibility of a softening of that person's paranoia. Instead, we typically see manifestations of rage that may well attend an increasing paranoia.

Impact on Gestalt Therapy Groups

Field theory tells us that that which occurs in one part of the field affects all other aspects of the field. Fairfield (2004, p. 340) quotes Parlett in stating that "a field is continuous in space and time." This means that our systems of support, our circles of friendship, love, and our physical environment, cannot be detached from malignancy at the top of the power structure—as distant as those power structures may appear to be. Our groups can and will be affected by what goes on at the top. On the other hand, those at the top may be affected, at least in some small way, by the work that we do. In a similar vein, field theory teaches us that *phenomena are determined by the whole field*. Group members will be affected by all that occurs in the greater field, and when leaders proclaim their prejudice against those in our groups who are most targeted: people of color, people with limited financial resources, sexual minorities, women and victims of sexual violence—those group members are likely going to feel an increased sense of vulnerability and anger in their lives and within our groups. Taking time to attend to these impacts are fundamental to effective, compassionate gestalt group therapy during periods of increased targeting of minority populations in the national political rhetoric.

Gestalt therapy is the quintessential anti-authoritarian form of psychotherapy. And, really, what could be more relevant to the current era, when nationalist and authoritarian leadership is on the rise internationally? All of Gestalt's founders, Frederick Perls, Laura Perls, and Paul Goodman, were politically progressive, and all were committed to the dignity of the individual in the face of oppressive social forces.

Fundamental to this anti- authoritarianism is that gestalt therapy supports the individual in using discrimination, aggression, and self-assertion to distinguish, on the one hand, between feelings and attitudes that are authentically one's own, and, on the other hand, feelings and attitudes that can more rightly be attributed to social norms or those belonging to old authority figures in one's history.

The boundary disturbance of *introjection* describes the process by which we absorb the preconceived ideas and prejudices of others as if they were our own. When powerful political leaders express a disdainful attitude toward women, Latinos, African Americans, or Muslims, it is easy to imagine that group members who feel themselves to be the object of these insults may become intimidated, feel frightened, or begin to internalize hateful projections. Toxic and hateful projections can be *introjected*, distort an individual's sense of self, and harm their capacity for self-activation. Much of the work of GGT is to help group members mobilize the self-support and anger needed to throw off such harmful projections. We refer to this process as *working through the introjects*. In the process of working through the introjects, the personal and the political often come together. In GGT, we create an environment of mutual support in which each group member has the opportunity to search for their own authentic voice, and the support to throw off the shackles of unhealthy projections and introjects. Group members who have been marginalized and who have become the objects of projection, are given support to find their agency and truth.

Under broad field conditions of rising oppression, the gestalt group becomes a place where group members can reflect on the situations they are facing—their fears, their hopes, their frustrations and their traumas. Whatever the field conditions may be, the gestalt group offers nothing utopian. We will always be constrained, and/or encouraged by conditions in the larger field. We offer no escape. What we do offer is support. When group members have the support of each other, then they can find the strength to survive periods of darkness, the courage to resist systems of oppression, and perhaps the will to organize opposition.

A Case Example

Our weekly group met on Wednesday, the day after the U.S. election. The seven group members who usually are very lively and glad to see each other in the waiting room were totally silent. They walked into the office looking as if they were walking into a funeral. Once the group began, a woman in her mid-thirties and Latina began to strongly cry. She expressed her fears about what is to come. As we went around the room, each person had their own feelings. A straight white man who is a journalist expressed fear about his profession, a lesbian expressed fears about hate crimes, a straight woman expressed fears about sexual assault. All group members expressed great sadness and dismay about the election and its outcome. As we connected with one another, the mood shifted. We were able to laugh a bit and even speak briefly of a few other topics, although we quickly reverted to the election and its impact on us. We agreed to support one another through all the difficulties that lay ahead.

A Reason for Hope

The journey to becoming a relatively free, autonomous and empowered human being is never easy. At the personal and collective level, we are sometimes beset with roadblocks, setbacks, injuries and relapses. There is no end to difficulty on this human journey. Yet, when we connect with one another, we can make meaning of our situation. We can find beauty in each other and in the world. We can learn and grow. We can resist the rise of fear and passivity in ourselves and our fellow human beings.

We can encourage creativity, love, compassion and resistance. We can be advocates for ourselves and others. We can give the support to each other that will be needed in order to go out into the world and be agents of change. This is the promise of gestalt group therapy, even in times like these. It is not a rose garden, but then again, it's not nothing.

References

Fairfield , M. A. (2004). Gestalt groups revisited: A phenomenological approach. *Gestalt Review*, 8 (3), 336–357.

Kernberg, O. (2004). *Aggressivity, narcissism, and self-destructiveness in the psychotherapeutic relationship*. New Haven, CT: Yale University Press.

Index

Author notes are indicated by 'n' and the note number after the page number e.g., 101n1.

introjection 38, 176
introjects, working through the 176–7
isolation 21, 45
I-Thou/I-It inter-human relations 17, 23, 25, 70, 81

Jacobs, Lynne 3, 8, 31, 60, 61
Johnson, Stephen 151

Kepner, Elaine, PhD 3
Kernberg, Dr. Otto 175

leader *see* group leader
leaders: boundary confusion of 84–6; vulnerabilities of ("shadow of the leader") 81–4
leadership types (group members): Defiant Leader 97; Emotional Leader 95, 96–7, 109; Scapegoat Leader 95–105, 108–11
leadership types (group members or group leaders): Task Leader 104n1
leadership/membership field: enactment 80–1; normalizing tensions 79–80; rupture and repair 78–9
leadership role, while maintaining dialogic stance 81–2
Lewin, Kurt 7, 9
Lichtenberg, Philip 95, 157–8, 160, 166
"Life Focus Communities" 159, 160–1, 170
listening 17, 37, 48–9, 49–50, 64, 159, 173
listening, to all voices in the field 91, 101, 164–6
lived experience, valuing of 10, 11, 17, 23, 154
long-term growth work 143–56
love-seeking 15

Manhattan (film) 22
meaning making 2, 10, 11, 12, 13, 26, 59, 177
member selection 89–92
members *see* group members
membership/leadership field *see* leadership/membership field
mobilization of energy 19, 51, 163
mutuality 29, 34

narratives 4, 13, 26, 64, 85, 141, 164–6; multiple narratives 91–4; personal 8

National Group Psychotherapy Institute, Washington 33
neuroscience 2
new equilibrium 19, 20, 51, 52

"Open Seat" method 3, 35, 41, 119
openness 10, 15, 17, 29, 34, 61, 80, 83

paradoxical theory of change 27–8, 33, 38, 52–3; definition of 52
passions 15, 39
patterning, laws of 12
perceptions 16, 57, 58, 79, 80, 84, 86, 162; construction of 11–13
Perls, Frederick ("Fritz"), MD 3, 53, 69, 119, 158–9; in the 1960s 7–8; in Frankfurt 11; friendship with Beisser 28; gestalt psychology and psychoanalysis, synthesis of 12; re-enactment of early life experiences 26
Perls, Laura, PhD 3, 7, 8, 92, 130; in Frankfurt 11; gestalt psychology and psychoanalysis, synthesis of 12
personal narrative 8
phenomenology 1, 4, 7, 10–11, 23; clinical 143, 154–5
philosophy of dialogue 1, 4
points of dialogue/inquiry 35
polarity 44, 45, 47, 53, 54, 61, 107, 144, 169
Polster, Erving 26, 70–1, 159, 160–1, 170
Polster, Miriam 171
power 83–4
presence 4, 24–5, 84, 101, 102, 112, 151–2, 162
process orientation 1, 33, 34
process-oriented gestalt group therapy 37–65
progressive psychoanalysis 1, 4, 7, 20, 158
projection 21–2, 38, 47–8, 58, 110–11, 176–7
psychotherapy 2–3, 4n1, 10, 33, 61, 84, 158–9, 163

relational/contactful position, tension with its opposite 37, 44–8, 92–3
relational development 31–67; definition of 31, 34; *intimately connected* aspect of 31, 34–5;

 Taylor & Francis eBooks

Helping you to choose the right eBooks for your Library

Add Routledge titles to your library's digital collection today. Taylor and Francis ebooks contains over 50,000 titles in the Humanities, Social Sciences, Behavioural Sciences, Built Environment and Law.

Choose from a range of subject packages or create your own!

Benefits for you

>> Free MARC records
>> COUNTER-compliant usage statistics
>> Flexible purchase and pricing options
>> All titles DRM-free.

REQUEST YOUR **FREE** INSTITUTIONAL TRIAL TODAY

Free Trials Available
We offer free trials to qualifying academic, corporate and government customers.

Benefits for your user

>> Off-site, anytime access via Athens or referring URL
>> Print or copy pages or chapters
>> Full content search
>> Bookmark, highlight and annotate text
>> Access to thousands of pages of quality research at the click of a button.

eCollections – Choose from over 30 subject eCollections, including:

Archaeology	Language Learning
Architecture	Law
Asian Studies	Literature
Business & Management	Media & Communication
Classical Studies	Middle East Studies
Construction	Music
Creative & Media Arts	Philosophy
Criminology & Criminal Justice	Planning
Economics	Politics
Education	Psychology & Mental Health
Energy	Religion
Engineering	Security
English Language & Linguistics	Social Work
Environment & Sustainability	Sociology
Geography	Sport
Health Studies	Theatre & Performance
History	Tourism, Hospitality & Events

For more information, pricing enquiries or to order a free trial, please contact your local sales team: www.tandfebooks.com/page/sales

Made in United States
Orlando, FL
03 November 2021